Wild Hog Hunting

By Craig Marquette
and Dave Sturkey

ISBN 0-9661183-0-8 19.95

Library of Congress
96-061091

Published by:

WILDLIFE PUBLISHING
622 Whitfield Ave.
Sarasota, FL 34243

Printed in the United States of America
First Edition
1 2 3 4 5 6 7 8 9 10

DEDICATION

To our supportive wives, who always smile when we come home successful, mourn when we don't, and never take any joy in our failures. Thanks for understanding our addiction to hunting, our love of the outdoors, and our need to share our stories with you (over and over again). Thanks for making home a place that we desire to be and hunting an activity that we enjoy, not an escape that we seek.

ACKNOWLEDGMENTS

The making of any book is a team effort. We acknowledge our fallible use of the wisdom of the following people. We would like to thank these friends for their help in this project.

Bill Frankenberger - a biologist for the state of Florida who answered every question and spent many hours with us and made himself available in every way. He treated us like beloved sons rather than those who were taking up too much of his time.

Keith Gosselin - a talented illustrator who worked to help us laugh at ourselves.

Tom McGee - a friend and wonderful photographer who helped to provide the pictures contained in this book.

Kathy Moore - a noble friend who with her helpful son Chris, spent two days with us and two dead hogs after Hurricane Danny to capture the cover photograph of this book.

Jerry Peoples - a professional trapper who shared with us his best-kept secrets and a lifetime of hunting and trapping experiences.

Craig Thompson - a great friend and hunting partner who helped write the chapters on field-dressing and cooking the wild hog. Craig was also involved in many of the hunts mentioned in the book!

Heidi Wile - a wonderful friend who proofread the text and helped with the grammar and spelling, something with which we rednecks sometimes struggle.

TABLE OF CONTENTS

HUNTING
URBAN
HUMANS

First Lessons with Wild Hogs

Chapter One

- *How difficult is hog hunting compared to other big-game hunting?*
- *What are some early hog hunting experiences of the author?*
- *What types of questions will be answered by this book?*

You can kill a hog! It's both the reason you bought this book and the reason I wrote it. Now, I don't say this to give you false hopes of success. I realize that there are many types of hunting that require linking an inexperienced hunter with a seasoned expert. Turkey and duck hunting are just two examples. Both require skills in calling and set-up that are almost impossible to acquire without finding a good mentor. Hunting hogs is not the same kind of challenge and requires skills that can be learned through trial and error, or more quickly, through the knowledge gained in this book.

My first memories of wild hogs come from my childhood years. Not that we had wild hogs in my region of Virginia, but the hunting magazines I read often spoke of the great adventure of wild boar hunting. "*Someday I will hunt wild boar*," I remember thinking as a young hunter. The tusks, the danger, the mysterious wild hog! Years of hunting deer, quail, turkey, dove, and other game filled my youth and teen years. Trips out west for mule deer and elk dominated my attention during my young adult days, but I never forgot those first impressions of wild hog hunting and my intention to someday hunt them.

When I moved to Florida, I set two hunting goals. The first was to kill an Osceola turkey, and the second was to learn how to hog hunt! On my first trip to interview for a new job in Sarasota, I made sure to stop in at the *Bullet Hole*, a local gun shop, and talk to the owner about hogs. Yes, I was told, hogs are everywhere in Florida and hunting areas are accessible. I took the job!

Where does one begin in hunting an animal that is totally foreign and new? Like everyone else, I began talking to people around me who had hunted hogs and seemed to be *in-the-know*. I learned a lot, just from the stories and experiences of others, but was left in confusion at times. It seemed that much of the information I learned from others was contradictory and doubtful. What was I supposed to believe?

The Noble but Much-Maligned Wild Hog

Statements that demonstrate that our beloved wild hog is under-appreciated.

"You smell like a pig"
"He's a real porker"
"You eat like a pig"
"Sucking last teat"
"In a pig's eye"
"Your room looks like a pigsty"
"Don't be a hog, share some with others"
"Crooked as a pig's tail"
"I'll do ________, when pigs fly"
"Putting your pearls before swine"
"Can't make a silk purse out of a sow's ear"
"Look at the snout on that sow"
"He's such a boar"
"The kid's a real ham"

When Would You Shoot?

Finally, the big day arrived when a friend invited me to be a guest on his private hunt club lease near Venice, Florida. We rode in a jeep half the morning and sighted no hogs. I wasn't used to *road* hunting, so I asked to be let out and allowed to still hunt through a certain hardwood section. I hadn't gone 100 yards from the jeep when I looked up to see a nice sow feeding across the creek. She noticed something unusual, probably my movement, and disappeared from sight! I didn't think she was extremely spooked, so I judged the direction of the wind and ran quickly ahead of her retreat path. I crossed the creek, went to kneeling position and waited.

Five minutes later I looked up to see her coming my way. My friend had told me that a 110-pound sow was a prime eating hog and she appeared to be in that range. At 50 yards I put the cross hairs below her ear and squeezed off a shot. She dropped like a sack of flour and didn't even kick. My first wild hog was down. I had killed a hog, but I didn't know anything about them.

I soon realized there was a world of knowledge I did not then possess. If I were ever to be an expert, I must not only kill hogs, but I must understand my quarry intimately. I had to answer such questions as: *What is a "wild" hog? Where did they come from? What are their habits and social life like? What do they eat? Do they vocalize like deer? Are they susceptible to "sow-in-heat" scent? How do you trap them? Were all the things I was hearing about hogs from others true? Were they dangerous? Did they attack? What is "dog hunting" all about? Are there special things to know for special weapons? What are the secrets to hunting them on public land? Where do they live and why? What do the "experts" do that average hunters know nothing about?*

As I began to search out the answers to these questions, the more I came to realize that there was no authoritative guide to help me learn about hogs. I began speaking with biologists, researchers, and expert hunters. I became more and more knowledgeable and skilled. This book is the result of those early questions and long years of study and personal experience. This is the first hog hunting book on the market! My thanks go to all those who have taught me and helped me. I've learned so much more than I ever dreamed was there and I know that by the end of this book - you will know more than 95% of all hunters and even guides of the wild hog. Almost every time I interact with experts or hunt for myself, I learn something new that makes me a better hunter. It is your job to take the knowledge gained in this book and learn to use it to be a more effective and responsible wild hog hunter. The information contained here will also help you to become a more skilled hunter for other big-game animals.

Marquette Brothers with Two Trophy Boars!

Handsome Fellow Ready for the Wall!

I'VE HEARD THE HUNTING IS GREAT IN AMERICA!
30-06

Wild Hog History

Chapter Two

- *What exactly is a "wild" hog?*
- *Where did "wild" hogs come from?*
- *What is the history of hogs once they were introduced into America?*

It had been a tough day conquering a new world! One thousand men began the exciting exploration into America. Dreams of treasures and gold-filled cities were foremost on each man's mind. Over the next river, through the next forest, across the next region lay all the riches a man could ever want. Poor men would live like kings. Rich men would gather fame. Everyone would be blessed! Explorers have three goals - stay alive, travel fast, and seek for the gold! When so motivated, men can move great distances through uncharted areas, even 400 years ago! Although the thousand men were eager to travel, they soon discovered a flaw in their plan. The swine they had brought along for food were not nomadic and could not be herded easily. Written in the journal of that first day of new world exploration were curses toward our beloved hog. The explorers made just over 3 miles in their first eager day of travel!

Domestic Hogs Gone Wild

The wild hog is a domestic hog gone wild. During the years of the early Spanish explorer, Hernando de Soto, domestic hogs escaped or were sold to Indians. A semi-wild population thus began to be established across the southern regions where de Soto traveled.

All wild hogs (scientific name "*Sus scrofa*") in the United States are "feral" animals (more details in chapter 3). Feral is a Latin term which means "fierce" or "wild." *It is a description used of domestic animals that have gone wild.* There are feral dog and cat populations in the United States, as well as "feral" cows. Feral cattle are like deer, harboring an intense fear of man and foraging completely for themselves. This is a common "feral" characteristic.

Both the early settlers and the Indians seem to have used the "open range" to keep their hogs since they had no truly effective fencing. The jump from domestic to wild was not a difficult one under these conditions!

Up until recently, *wild* hogs on *public* land could be claimed by individuals as their own private livestock. This practice was known as *"hog claims"* or *"hog rights."* Hogs were thus allowed to run wild and were only occasionally rounded up or captured for slaughter or market. This practice continued for more than four hundred years.

To "claim" a hog as your own on public lands, you simply trapped a wild hog and placed a registered notch on his ear. Many people had traps located on public forest lands, and whenever a hog was trapped, it was either marked then released or taken home for food! During hard times, hogs were rounded up and the marketable hogs were separated from those not worthy of selling. Wild hogs were a major "food" and economic source for many farmers and old-timers. One old-timer told me that through the depression, many of the country people lived on the hogs that they ranged on public land. Wild hog was often the only meat on the table!

In 1966, the *United States Forest Service* declared that free-ranging practices would no longer be allowed in Florida. Other states did the same thing at different times. All those who claimed ownership of hogs on public property were asked to remove their hogs. After an extended amount of time, the government then stopped allowing these "owners" the right to access their hogs on public lands. To stop any chance of feuding, professional trappers were hired to capture the remaining hogs and to sell them back to the owners. Those that were not claimed were sold or slaughtered.

Places Named After Hogs

Hog Back Mountain, SC
Hog Canyon, England
Hog Creek, TX
Boarhills, Scotland
Hog Eye, AR
Hog Island, GA
Hog Point, VA
Hog Head, Ireland
Hog's Back, England
Pigs Peak, South Africa
Pig, VA
Bay of Pigs, Cuba
Sow River, England
Hog Scald Hollow, AR

This caused goodwill among those who had been disappointed with the new laws forbidding free range, because the professionals caught many hogs that would never have been claimed otherwise.

Details of Hog Introduction into the New World

The wild hog came originally from Europe, then to Cuba and the surrounding areas with the early explorers. As a matter of fact, his history is directly connected to ole Christopher Columbus. Columbus, on his second voyage in 1493, brought just "eight" domestic swine with him to be released into the West Indies for food stock for future voyagers.

The hogs were often, on these islands, left to forage for themselves and ran wild. Reportedly, in just 13 years, the colonists that introduced the hogs to these areas were forced to begin hunting them. There are early reports of two major problems. The hogs were supposedly so aggressive that they

Hernando's Herd

killed cattle and also attacked people at times. The crop destruction of maize and sugarcane probably proved to be an even greater problem. The ancient problem was the same as the modern, the wild hog destroyed crops, habitat, and competed with native species for food. Hunting then, like today, was the answer!

Details of Hog Introduction into the United States

The Spanish explorer, Hernando de Soto, captured some of these hogs left in Cuba and the West Indies by Columbus and took them to the United States.[1] His mission was to explore the Spanish claimed region of Florida and then to head west! He was declared "governor" by emperor Charles V and sent to search for treasure and the legendary land of great riches. He brought 1,000 men with him and landed in 1539 at Charlotte Harbor, Florida.

De Soto sent his ships back to Cuba so that his men would have nothing that would encourage them to desert their mission. They explored present day Florida, South Carolina, North Carolina, Alabama, Mississippi and other regions. De Soto discovered the Mississippi River in 1541 and then crossed over into Arkansas, Oklahoma, and Texas. After finding no treasure, and traveling more than 3,000 miles, de Soto died on the journey back to the Spanish settlements located on the Gulf of Mexico in 1542. Some of his men survived. I can't show you a direct human descendant from de Soto, but the woods are full of his swine descendents.

[1] There is some debate concerning whether De Soto introduced the hogs or whether Ponce de Leon introduced them, at the same site, 15 years earlier. This expedition is not well-documented, and therefore the certainty of hog introduction at this time cannot be authenticated. Since Ponce de Leon was killed as soon as he set foot on Florida, it is likely that these swine were never unloaded from the ships and returned to Cuba instead.

Hogs created problems soon after their introduction into Cuba and the West Indies, and hogs quickly became a problem in America too. On the first day of travel, de Soto reported in his journal of making only 3.5 miles because the 13 sows (males were not mentioned in the count) were so uncooperative. He probably at times regretted his plan to use the hogs for food for his men and wondered whether they were worth the effort (the hogs, of course, not the men). He left many of the hogs at the settlements he established along the way.

Food had been a major problem of previous explorers and the swine multiplied quickly. A year after de Soto came to the United States, the 13 original sows had increased to approximately 300 hogs. From these hogs came the wild hog of the continental United States.

De Soto's Descendants

The hogs present in the United States today are not all descended from de Soto's pigs. Other people have released different types of hogs over the past 400 years. Sometimes this was intentional, sometimes not! The great majority, though, are descended directly from de Soto. The results of these other introductions are the subject of the next chapter.

The Beauty of the Hunt!

I DONT KNOW IF MY FATHER WILL APPROVE OF ME DATING A RUSSIAN

The Identification of the Wild Hog

Chapter Three

- *What is the difference between a wild hog and a javelina?*
- *What are the four types of hogs (three types of wild hogs)?*
- *What are general characteristics (color, size, diet) of hogs?*
- *What is a trophy boar?*

Ben stood victoriously over his newly harvested wild hog! He knew that it was a boar hog but how was one to judge it? It looked big, but how big was it in comparison to other hogs? Was it a trophy boar? What kind of hog had he killed? Was it a Russian Boar like many of the magazines often advertised? Ben realized that his story to his friends would be mostly the guesses and opinions of a novice hog hunter. This chapter will help you relay the proper facts along with any embellishments that you might want to add on your own!

Types of Pigs Found In the World

There are two families of pig-like mammals found in the world. There are the Old World Pigs (Suidae) and the Peccaries (Tayassuidae). There are five types of Old World Pigs (bush pig, **wild boar**, wart hog, giant forest pig, and babirusa) with eight species and seventy-six subspecies. Javalinas are in the peccary family and not directly related to wild hogs. Javalinas populate Texas, Arizona, New Mexico, California, and Mexico, as well as other areas. They have many of the same characteristics of hogs, but are much smaller. Hunting javalina is a great western past-time! Wild hogs are in the other family, Suidae.

American wild hogs come from either domestic hogs or actual "Wild Boar" strains that have been introduced here. Since the domestic hog is a direct, but distant, descendant of the Wild Boar, they are very similar in both genetics and habits (which means they can interbreed).

All pigs are social (they have clearly defined roles and interaction), non-ruminant (they do not chew the cud like cows), ungulate (hooved animals - be sure to see the diagram showing the difference between deer and hog tracks), omnivores (they eat both animal matter and vegetation).

They all have a wide variety of foods that they will eat. Because much of their food is found below ground, pigs root (dig with their nose) and have a great sense of smell. Eyesight in all swine is very poor but hearing is acute. Hogs are also highly intelligent animals. If you remember watching the old TV program, Green Acres, you will recall that Arnold could do most any trick that a dog could perform!

Types of Hogs Found In the United States

There are four types of hogs present in the United States today. They are the "Russian Wild Boar", the "Domestic Hog", the "Feral Hog", and the "Hybrid Hog." Every hog you see in the United States will be one of these distinct four types.

Russian WildBoar

"Eurasian Wild Boar"

Russian Boar with characteristic grizzled face.

Some say that Russian Wild Boar are the meanest, baddest, and toughest hogs in the world! A more proper name of "Russian Wild Boar" is "Eurasian Wild Boar." This is a more accurate term because Russian Wild Boar come from many places other than Russia. They are found in Europe, Asia, and Africa. There are many subspecies of Eurasian Boar, but they are all somewhat similar.

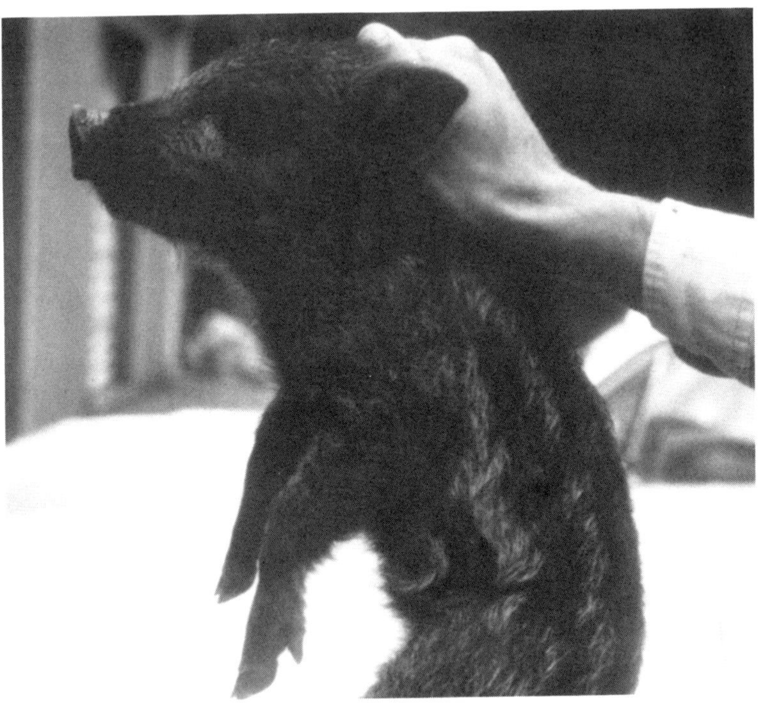

Watermelon striped Russian piglet.

Eurasian wild boar begin life as "watermelon striped" piglets. Many hunters, when they find a watermelon striped piglet, claim a genetic link to Eurasian wild boar. This is improper. Researchers believe that the striped piglets can be found in "feral" populations where Eurasians have not been introduced. In other words, all Eurasian Boar are striped, although some pure feral hogs have this genetic characteristic. Eurasians start off life as striped, light red or brown, shoats (another word for piglet) and turn red tinted, grizzled, and darker as they get older. Eurasian wild boar have a more consistent coloring than any of the other three types of hogs.

True Russian Wild Boar tend to have longer legs, a more sloped back, and a straighter tail than feral hogs. By far they have the longest snout of the four types of hogs. The most striking difference is seen in the hair. Mature Eurasian hogs have white-tipped hairs on their face and along their mouth region. They also have multiple split-ends. Old boars get a white grizzled look to them. There is a more pronounced raised hair region along the snout (near the mouth line).

Eurasian wild boar are more aggressive than feral hogs. Since they have never become domesticated, they have a deeper wild "streak" within them. I know a professional feral hog trapper who was invited by a wildlife park to take their extra Eurasian hogs. He brought them to his pens and isolated them from his feral hogs. After a week of isolation, he introduced a feral hog into the large enclosure holding the Eurasian hogs. The Eurasian hogs killed the feral hog and then ate him!

From this story you can learn something that is accurate and assume something that is not. It is accurate that Eurasian wild hogs are more aggressive than all other hogs. For this reason, Eurasian wild boar are very difficult to keep in captivity. Sows often eat their own young if kept in captivity (that makes breeding them in captivity difficult).

However, it would be a wrong assumption that feral hogs and Eurasians do not interact and interbreed with each other. I have been under a feeder with a group of half-tamed wild feral and Eurasian boar. Both types interacted as equals. I did notice that the feral piglets watched me when I moved, but the Russian piglets ran from me and returned only after I settled down. There is a greater "wildness" in the Russian breed, evident even in their young.

There are probably NO RUSSIAN WILD BOAR in the wild anywhere in the United States. Pure Russian Boar are probably found on only a few private hunting preserves if at all. All have most likely interbred with the resident feral populations in the wild or had hybrids introduced into their midst.

There are many "Russian" characteristics found in wild populations because Russian boar have been introduced into many feral populations. These hogs with Russian characteristics should not be confused with pure strain Russians, they are "hybrids" (see section on hybrids). For "pure" strains of Russian boar to exist, they must be isolated from feral or hybrid hog populations. All wild hogs are very similar and an equal challenge, even if they are not pure Russian Boar!

Domestic Hogs

Hundreds of Different Breeds

The first domestication of the pig is thought to have taken place in China around 4,900 BC and may have occurred as early as 10,000 BC in Thailand. Domestic pigs are the largest of the four types of hogs. They come in more than 377 varieties. Domestics are much larger than their wild cousins. Some types of domestic boars can reach more than 2,000 pounds. Average domestic boars weigh near 700 pounds, whereas a healthy feral boar generally weighs less than 200. This great difference is primarily because of selective breeding, a lack of parasites in domestics, and a much greater availability of food. Through selective breeding and genetic research, improvements are constantly being made! Can you imagine a "cholesterol free" pig? Researchers at some of our greatest universities are working on these kinds of projects.

There are three major types of domestic pigs: the lard, the meat, and the bacon types. Lard pigs have a higher percentage of fat

Domestic Hogs Grow Large Through Selective Breeding

than the other two types. Meat pigs have less fat than lard pigs, but more than bacon type pigs. Bacon pigs have the least amount of body fat.

Landrace pigs produce the highest quality bacon and are solid white with long ears. Berkshire pigs are an excellent meat pig and have a black coat with white on it's feet, face, and tail tip. The Duroc is a red pig and the Hampshire pig is the most popular pig in the United States.

Pigs are used for a number of things other than food. High quality leather, durable bristles for many kinds of brushes, as well as hundreds of medical products and research are some of the many uses of pigs. The first human heart replacement valves were made from pig valves. Many people who have pig valves in their hearts report an inability to eat barbeque or pass a slaughter house without crying (I'm kidding!). In southern France though,

Feral Sow

domesticated hogs are trained to find truffles (a mushroom like delicacy) because of their great sense of smell.

On today's hog farms, hogs reach slaughter size in just 5-6 months. At that time, the average weight of a domestic pig will be approximately 225-250 pounds. Domestic sows normally give birth to 8-14 piglets and most of these survive because of measures taken by the breeders to protect them from being hurt by adult hogs.

"Pigs" are those swine up to 120 pounds, and "hogs" are those more than 120 pounds. Hunters use the terms "pig" and "hog" interchangeably, as well as other names such as "rooter" and "razorback".

Another interesting fact to note is that there is no other domesticated animal that so easily and quickly returns to a wild state. Domestic hogs become wild hogs very easily!

Feral Hogs

THE WILD HOG YOU WILL MOST OFTEN SEE!

Feral hogs are generally heavy and stocky with a dense coat of bristly hair, short legs, and a long snout (although not as long as Russian or Hybrid strains). They come in many colors, but black, red, and multicolored are predominant. When compared to deer of the same weight, hogs are much shorter and rounded. The male and female hog have "tusks" (female tusks are shorter) which are lower canine teeth that grow long. The top canine teeth are called "whetters" and sharpen the tusks (lower canines) as the hog chews. Boars sometimes "pop" the two together when they are being aggressive.

Feral hogs are domestic hogs gone wild. They are the predominant wild hog found in the United States. Sixteen states have huntable wild hog populations, including Hawaii (in Hawaii, hogs were introduced before de Soto introduced hogs into southern regions).

Feral hogs and domestic hogs are more than closely related cousins. They are the same animal. The things that farmers do for hogs (feed and choose breeding mates) are now done by the hogs themselves.

You might not believe that the feral is a domestic gone wild because of several differences. Domestics have little hair while feral hogs have a thick coat. Domestic pigs have tons of fat while feral hogs have little. Most domestic hogs have small or no tusks (usually because they're removed or the males are castrated at a young age), while feral boars generally possess a visible tusk.

Why do the ferals and domestics look so different if they are the same animal? It's really quite simple. Domestic pigs are "selectively" bred to produce certain desirable characteristics. If you were to stop this selective breeding, the specialized domestic hog becomes a mutt! Why don't you find German Shepherds, Dalmatians, Poodles, or Spaniels in wild dog populations? Simply because when dogs get together, they breed with anyone and everyone and these specialized traits are hidden in the genetic pool. The same is true with wild hogs. Feral hogs are simply mutts!

The life span of feral hogs, in unhunted populations, is about 8-12 years. Over time, and depending on the diet of the hog in a specific area, they will lose their teeth or suffer from severe gum disease. As the hog becomes less able to feed, he becomes stressed and is more susceptible to disease and predators. This is the way that most older hogs die.

Mature feral hogs average between 20-30 inches at the shoulder. Healthy males average around 150 pounds or slightly more. Females average slightly less than this, near 140 pounds. Castrated males (barrows) can reach into the 300+ pound range. Tremendously large hogs are sometimes shot (some near 800 pounds), but these tend to be fed on feeders at game farms or only a generation or two from being domestic. If you capture hogs, castrate and vaccinate them for parasites, and turn them loose, their weights will dramatically increase. Most well run hunting clubs can maintain boars in the mid-200 range by castration and feeding programs. True wild hogs, unsupported by man's efforts, can't reach this kind of weight because of parasites, the energy necessary to obtain food, and the energy spent mating.

An interesting fact concerns the famous Arkansas Razorback. It is not a "Russian Wild Boar" but simply the same feral hog found throughout other wild hog regions. Russian Wild Boar were never introduced into Arkansas, although Florida, Texas and Maine, as well as a few other regions, have some history of Russian

(Eurasian) introduction. Tennessee Russian Boar are hybrid hogs that have a strong Eurasian (Russian) background. Tennessee has no feral hogs, only hybrids, and is very rare in this respect.

Hybrid Hogs

Russian Wild Boar Crossed with Feral Hogs

Hybrid hogs are a cross between feral hogs and Eurasian or Russian Wild Boar. Since there have been so few Eurasian Wild Boar introduced into the United States, most hybrids are predominately feral pigs. The hybrid does carry distinctive characteristics from the gene pool of the Eurasian Wild Boar. Hybrids tend to have a longer snout than feral hogs, but shorter than pure Eurasians. They also have the distinctive white bristle-tipped hair coloration in the facial region like the pure Eurasian. Hybrid piglets are often striped but this is also sometimes a naturally occurring phenomenon in pure feral hog populations.

285 Pound Hybrid Boar

Anywhere true Russian Boar have been introduced into the wild, hybrid characteristics can be found. In Florida, for example, this means that three areas are most likely to hold hybrids - Avon Park Air Force Range, J.W. Corbett Game Management Area, and Eglin Air Force Base. In Texas, Russian Boar were introduced into Calhoun County, on the Edwards Plateau, and in the Rio Grande valley. While researching this book, I met many individuals who have introduced Eurasian Wild Boar in other areas onto their private leases and this has been unreported to game authorities (it is also highly unlikely that these were totally pure Eurasians, even though those who introduced them may have thought so). See end of chapter for a list of states with wild hogs and types of hogs present.

GENERAL QUESTIONS CONCERNING HOG IDENTITY!

Are there different species of wild hogs that have neck waddles or mule feet?

Many old-timers swear that these characteristics are common to a different species of wild hog, but they are not. Neck waddles are elongated growths of skin in the neck region. Mule feet are where the hoof of the hog is a singular unit instead of the common two-part hoof. Both of these characteristics are caused by recessive genes and are rare but found in all wild hog populations.

What is a shield, and are there differences in shields in the different types of hogs?

A shield is a thick layer of tissue located on the sides of the shoulders of boar hogs. Eurasian wild boar have thicker shields than feral hogs - up to 3 inches or more in thickness! Shields are secondary sexual characteristics (like tusks). Their thickness is determined by the age of the hog. Castration causes loss or incomplete shield development. See the chapter on special weapons hunting for a more in-depth analysis of shields and measures needed to overcome them.

What is a "trophy" boar?

The Safari Club International defines a trophy boar as one with tusks at least 1 and 1/4 inches long. The hog doesn't have to be the baddest hog with a mean attitude to qualify as a trophy. Hogs weighing over 200 pounds are great hogs. All hogs, even boar, can be good eating, but some very large boars can also be rancid in taste.

STATES WHICH HAVE WILD HOGS

•**Alabama** - Feral and Hybrids are present in the state. Hybrids are very rare, if they occur at all. They are found mostly in the counties near the confluence of the Tombigbee and Alabama rivers. In earlier years, hogs could be hunted throughout the year and without limit.

•**Arizona** - Only Feral hogs are present in the state. They are located in a few areas, but are only thought to be "common" in the Havasu National Wildlife Refuge. The population is hunted annually and does not appear to be expanding.

•**Arkansas** - Only Feral hogs are present in the state. They are found along the areas surrounding the Ouachita River watershed, Cossatot River, and along the southern half of the state along the Mississippi River bottom lands. There are huntable populations present.

•**California** - Feral and Hybrids are present in the state. Eurasian Wild Boar were introduced in Tehama County at Dye Creek Ranch in 1968. In 1925, they were introduced in Monterey County, and in 1940 they were introduced into Santa Barbara County.

•**Florida** - Feral and Hybrids are present in the state. Wild hogs are found in every county of the state. In the 1986-87 season, about 50,000 hogs were harvested. The greatest numbers of hogs are found in the south central Florida and along the northern Gulf coast of the state. Three fourths of all wild hogs live in Florida and Texas.

•**Georgia** - Feral and Hybrids are present in the state. They are found in the coastal plain and in the extreme northern mountain areas, as well as in limited areas in the Piedmont section. In the 1950's, Russian Boar were introduced into Towns, Rabun, Murray, and Gilmer counties.

•**Hawaii** - Feral hogs only are present in the state. They exist on all the major islands of Hawaii and are causing tremendous damage to the habitat.

•**Iowa** - There was once a wild hog population, but they have been eliminated from the state.

•**Kentucky** - Feral and Hybrids are present in the state. Only a few hogs are found in the south-central part of the state. There are scattered populations in Marion, Estill, Lee, Wayne, and McCreary counties.

•**Louisiana** - Feral and Hybrids are present in the state. They are mostly present in the central and southwestern portions of the state. They do occur in other areas.

•**Mississippi** - Feral and Hybrids are present in the state. They are found mainly in the counties bordering the Mississippi and Pearl rivers in the southeastern corner of the state. Hybrids have not been scientifically confirmed as existing in the state.

•**Missouri** - There was once a wild hog population in Missouri, but they have been eliminated from the state.

•**New Hampshire** - Only Hybrids or Pure Eurasians exist in the state. These are located in Corbin's Park and the surrounding areas where they have escaped. Feral hogs have never been present, but Hybrids were introduced to interbred with the resident Eurasian population. They can be hunted.

•**New Mexico** - Only Feral hogs only are present in the state. They occur mostly in Hidalgo County.

•**North Carolina** - Feral and Hybrids are present in the state. They are present mostly in the southwestern mountain region and the Hybrids are predominant. In the eastern part of the state, feral hogs are reported. There are high populations in the extreme southeastern part of Virginia and are probably present across the border in this area of North Carolina.

•**Oklahoma** - Feral hogs only are present in the state. There is a small and probably decreasing population.

•**Oregon** - There was once a wild hog population in Oregon, but they have been eliminated from the state.

•**South Carolina** - Feral and Hybrids are present in the state. They are found mostly in the river system areas and along the lower coastal plain.

•**Tennessee** - Hybrids only are present in the state. The majority of hybrids are located in the southeastern corner of the state in Polk, Monroe, Blount, and Sevier counties. They are also found in the Cumberland Plateau. They are also found in Lauderdale County.

•**Texas** - Feral and Hybrids are present in the state. They are very numerous and occur in the southeastern, central, and southwestern portions of the state. The herd is currently expanding. Three fourths of all wild hogs in the United States live in Texas and Florida.

•**Virginia** - Feral hogs only are present in the state. Hogs occur mainly in Princess Anne County in the extreme southeastern corner of the state. There is probably a total population of 400-500 animals.

•**Washington** - There was once a wild hog population, but they have been eliminated from the state.

•**West Virginia** - Hybrid hogs only are present in the state. They are present in Boone, Logan, and Wyoming counties in the mountains of these areas.

You're going to lose your lip!!
REDHOG
CHEWING TOBACCO

Wild Hog Habits

Social Habits, Hunting Hot Spots, Communication, and General Questions

Chapter Four

- *What are the social structures and habits of hogs?*

- *What do wild hogs eat? Where do hogs spend their time?*

- *What vocalizations do hogs use to communicate?*

- *How do boars change their habits after being castrated?*

The Social World of the Hog

The basic social unit in the world of hogs is a sow and her litter. Sows also tend to gather with other females and their litters. Males have a greater tendency of being solitary, although it is not extremely unusual to find them with others. In a study done on Merritt Island National Wildlife Refuge in Florida, females were sighted with their young-of-the-year 75% of the time. Males were solitary 71% of the time. This means that most single animals you see are males and most in groups are females.

Hogs, when they are together, are normally found in groups (called *herds* or *sounders*) of not more than 8-10 individuals. In a study done at Fish Eating Creek near Palmdale, Florida, the average group size was 3. This is in line with my own field observations.

The social world of hogs is somewhat different from the social world of deer. A deer's mating season is over a very short period of time (generally two weeks of high intensity breeding) while sows come into heat year-round. This means that deer tend to aggressively defend a territory to maintain breeding dominance. Boars do not defend a breeding territory but battle for females whenever they come into heat on an individual basis.

Although hog mating occurs throughout the year, there are two peaks where the majority of breeding occurs. The greater peak takes place in the Fall when the acorns (mast) begin to drop. A smaller breeding peak occurs during the Spring green-up.

Biologist Bill Frankenberger believes that sex is the predominant drive in boars, even taking precedence over food. *Like the average man, your average boar loves to eat, but is willing to forgo a meal to chase a skirt when available.*

The gestation period of the sow is 115 days. Near the end of this time, the sow will build a nest. Can you believe that piglets come into the world in a nest? The nest is a depression on the ground that is furnished and layered with grasses, pine needles, or other available vegetation. A common feature of hog nests is the presence of some type of overhanging branch or cover.

Wild hogs generally have 4-8 piglets (the record for a domestic sow is 37). During the early part of their life, the piglets stay in the nest. Piglets have an extremely high mortality rate, as much as 40% die before reaching maturity. Piglets are very susceptible to

Almost Weaned!

cold, parasites, and predators. Their body heat is regulated by close proximity with the other piglets in the nest.

Within a few days, the piglets begin to follow the sow. They live mostly on the sow's milk, but also supplement this with solid foods almost immediately. Almost immediately after birth, there are fights to determine a pecking order. These fights determine a "teat order" among the piglets. Not all of the sow's teats produce milk at first or the same amounts of milk. The dominant piglets get the better teats. They are weaned about 8 weeks after birth (after weaning, they are called *shoats*)! This means that piglets can survive at 8 weeks, before this, you should not shoot the sow.

As hogs mature, there is a dominance structure that becomes fixed. Dominance controls priority of access to resources such as food, water, wallows, beds and mates. Males tend to exhibit dominant behavior with other males and females with other females but rarely with each other (marriage counselors would go out of business if this were true of humans). My trapper friends who sometimes raise a wild piglet tell me that they believe the females are much more dominant and will bite faster than the males. As the shoats near maturity, the sow becomes more and more aggressive with her young, attempting to drive them away before her next breeding season begins. Shoats mature and reach breeding age in about 6-8 months. At this time the process begins again with the sow. Sows generally only have one litter per year, although a common myth is that they have two or more litters a year.

When a boar is castrated and becomes a "bar" hog (technically *"barrow"*), his life is literally turned upside down. As the boar looses interest in finding and attracting females, he becomes a "coach potato" and eats way too many chips (one old-timer told me that stale potato chips are deadly bait for traps)! Bars are therefore much larger than boars and can be found in groups since the breeding drive is absent and maintaining dominance is unnecessary.

Truly big boars that are killed in the wild are usually castrated by man or something has gone wrong with their testicles naturally. Their energy is conserved and their attention is focused primarily on food, not sex! Bars often become "very" nocturnal. If someone castrated me during daylight, I might become nocturnal too! This explains the difficulty of killing a truly trophy "bar" hog. When boars are castrated, their tusks grow thicker. Many times, hunt clubs will cut the tip of the ear off the boars that they castrate, so that hunters can tell which is the better eating wild hogs on their property.

FOUR HUNTING HOT SPOT LOCATIONS

HOT SPOT ONE

WALLOWS

Wallows are shallow depressions in mud or low water where hogs will lay and roll around, covering themselves with a thick coating of mud. Wallows are the "bug spray" centers for pigs. The main purpose of the wallow is to keep external parasites from contacting the skin.

Wallows are easy to find and a good place to setup a stand because multiple hogs tend to use the same wallow. When bugs are bothering you, bugs are probably bothering your local swine population too!

In really fresh wallows, look for hair, snout, and hoof imprints.

Another purpose of wallows is to cool off. This is a secondary use for hogs. After a hard day at the office, in the heat of the day, hogs will wallow to relax and cool down. Rather than a pool loving yuppie, hogs are a mud loving red-neck! Hogs can swim well and often do swim in the swamps and rivers where I hunt. They are only hesitant to swim where gators are present.

All this means that wallows are probably good areas for stand hunting in the heat of the day and in the evening when the local bug population becomes active. Much of wallowing activity probably occurs at night, but daytime action is worth checking out!

HOT SPOT TWO

Rubbing Posts

Hogs like to rub against trees and posts. They use these to scratch themselves and to knock off external parasites and mud. Hogs carry a large number of external parasites (like ticks) and scratching becomes a common habit. Hogs rub on different trees and posts along their routes, but will also find a favorite place at times.

When walking through the woods, or riding the roads, keep your eyes open for blackened trees or posts. This lets you know that hogs are in the area and indicates common travel routes being used. The more rubbed posts, the greater the use of the area or trail. Since much of hog territory floods at times, it is important to be able to distinguish rubs from high-water flood marks.Flood marks on trees are generally brown and found on every tree at the same height. Hog rubs are only on certain trees and are black or darker than flood stains, although sometimes very similar.

Another interesting thing to look for when scouting is to notice the height of the "lichens" around the trees. Lichens are brightly colored growths on trees that look like mold! It does not grow below the high flood level marks on trees. This is a good way to

Look for rubbing posts with tusk marks.

judge how high water typically gets during the late summer and early fall flood season of your hunting land. There is nothing more discouraging that finding great hog habitat but being unable to access it during fall hunting. I generally find a low water area and a high water area with good hog concentrations. That way I am prepared to hunt no matter the weather!

Rub posts can tell you two very important things! First, they can tell you when hogs are using your area. If you find rubbing posts near a water crossing or exiting a swamp, it is easy to check these trees to see "when" they are wet. Hogs exiting the swamp will be wet and the rubbing posts will be wet also. Wet or dry rubbing posts can also tell you the direction that hogs are traveling (wet posts indicate hogs leaving swamp areas; dry posts indicate swamp entrance points). Boars may use their tusks to mark their rubbing posts. This isn't always done but is a common enough behavior to watch for if you are "trophy boar" hunting. This will tell you about the presence of boar in your immediate vicinity!

HOT SPOT THREE

Resting Areas

Hog resting areas are places that hogs seek to sleep, lounge, and hide. Hogs, like deer, are looking for security! Resting sites typically are "thickly vegetated" areas that are difficult to access quietly. Hogs seek areas to rest where they can be aware of anyone's approach while they sleep and rest. These areas tend to be near feeding areas. If you find a fresh feeding area, look for the thickest areas adjacent to it. These are most likely the resting areas of these hogs. You are likely to find hogs located there during the day!

During parts of the year, hogs can be found active throughout the day. As temperatures rise or as hunting pressure increases, hogs will retreat to secure areas during the middle of the day. **These two factors, heat and pressure, determine the extent of daytime activity.** Early season hogs will be active throughout the day, but as the season progresses the activity will be more and more limited to morning and evening. **Hunting pressure determines the thickness of the area chosen to rest while heat determines the type of habitat sought**.

During cool winter or overcast days, hogs can be found resting in the middle of palmetto fields. On especially cold days hogs will try to rest in the sun! If the day is hot, shade becomes an important factor. On hot days, look for thick brushy areas that offer lots of shade. Also, on hot days, look for thick areas adjacent to water or wallows.

One of my favorite ways to hunt hogs is to slowly still hunt through swampy areas that have recently become dry. If you see low lying ferns - these are sometimes great resting areas. More than one hunter has told me that finding a sleeping buck is almost impossible, but putting a bullet into a sleeping boar can be done!

HOT SPOT FOUR

FEEDING AREAS

It will be no surprise to you to learn that hogs like to eat. As a tour guide at Myacca River State Park in Florida told me, "they will eat anything that won't eat them first." The variety of the hog's diet is intimidating until you understand the big picture and general categories that make up their diet.

Let's talk first about the categories of the hog's menu. Hog's, like humans, eat both meat and vegetation. They are "omnivores." Hogs are monogastric, which means they must gather their amino acids (protein) through animal matter. Hogs gain this needed protein by eating both living and dead animals and bugs.

Yes, hogs even eat carrion. One hog hunting video used dead hogs as bait for other hogs. One researcher told me that he thought they ate less carrion than was sometimes believed. Since hogs get the animal content of their diet primarily through invertebrates (bugs, worms, and grubs), he thought that hogs might be eating maggots rather than carrion much of the time. I have noticed hogs eating freshly killed animals and believe that carrion is a part of their diet whenever available.

Pickerel Weed has purple bloom in season.

Most animal matter in the hog's diet comes from invertebrates (commonly known as bugs). Hogs love bugs! Grubs, worms, and anything else they can catch is quickly eaten. A lot of rooting is done for this purpose. In winter, when plants are not growing and acorns have stopped falling, hogs root a great deal more than the rest of the year.

Hogs will also kill and eat small animals. Reptiles are a favorite, especially snakes. Wild hogs will even tangle with rattlesnakes. I haven't spoken to anyone who has seen a hog get the worse end of the deal. Snake venom is probably toxic in hogs, but the thick skin and coat prevents the snakes venom from being effective. Not enough venom is transferred to hurt the hog. If anyone has a different explanation or a story of just such an encounter, I'd love for you to contact me and let me know.

In Texas, hogs are currently the third major predator of lambs and baby goats. Coyotes are number one, bobcats are second, and

Asiatic Pennywort can be found in either water or land.

wild hogs are third. Once a hog learns that he can kill and eat a certain animal, he becomes a predator of that animal. Hogs also eat eggs and chicks of ground nesting birds as well as anything else that he can catch.

Animal matter makes up a different percentage of the hogs diet depending on the season, but generally only about 10% of his diet is found in this category. On the average, vegetation makes up about 90% of the hog's diet.

During the fall and winter, 99% of the hog's vegetable diet is made up of acorns, cabbage palm seeds *(sabal palmetto)*, and citrus! Yep, it's hard to believe, but hogs love orange juice. Any wild citrus tree in the woods is worth checking out.

In the spring and summer, the majority of the hog's vegetable diet (90%) is concentrated on foliage/herbage and roots/stems. The primary types include various grasses (*gramineae*), pickerel weed (*pontederia sp.*), and asiatic pennywort (*centella asiatica*). Secondary food sources include various leaves, bulbs, mushrooms, and tubers.

The beginning of fall brings a dramatic change in the hog's diet. The hog goes from eating no fruits and seeds to these making up more than 60% of his diet. **There is a tremendous migration to oak tree areas for this reason in the fall.** I have noticed that an oak area will have no hog activity one weekend and be overrun the next weekend. A few years ago one of my friends put up two ladder stands in a favorite oak hammock and found absolutely no evidence of hogs. The next weekend he saw more than 30 hogs from one of these stands. Individual oak trees will begin to drop acorns sooner than others. Find these early trees and you can be in for some great hunting. Hogs also eat agricultural crops including corn, milo, wheat, rice, soybeans, peanuts, potatoes, watermelons, and cantaloupe. Hogs will eat other crops too.

Hog Communication 101

Hogs communicate in a variety of ways. Communication is important because hogs are social animals, preferring to keep in contact with other hogs. In a study done in 1958, more than 60 types of communication signals were classified, but only a few will be mentioned for our purposes of hunting here! The knowledge gained in this portion of the book will help you identify hog sounds and communications in the woods and know what's going on!

Visual Signals

All visual signals identified within wild hog populations seem to be related to aggression activity. Visual signals are threats! Hogs are partial to body language and bluff.

Notice the raised hair on the spinal region to find the dominant sow!

The "lateral"or "broadside" signal is a threat where a hog comes alongside another and moves his head as if to slash his opponent. The hairs along the spinal region of a hog stand on end as a further sign of aggression. When sows are feeding together, you can even tell the dominant sow by this raised hair signal. Wild hogs will also strut in a stiff-legged manner with head lowered as a sign of domination.

Auditory Signals

There are four major types of audible signals used by hogs.

- **LOCATION GRUNTS**

When hogs are walking through the forest in a social group, they often keep in contact with each other with soft grunts repeated often. When still hunting through thick areas, I have often heard these grunts as I approached within yards of feeding hogs. If you can hear these soft grunts, hogs are within range.

- **DISTRESS CALLS**

Hogs, when alarmed, sometimes use calls to warn others of impending doom! This call is a "huff" when the unknown object is sighted and determined to be dangerous. It is a low pitched, loud grunt according to researcher Daniel Baber. I think it sounds like a "huff" which is quickly followed by the quick retreat of wild hogs.

One morning last year while sitting on my stand, I heard a nearby shotgun. The morning stillness was broken by a piercing squeal of a wounded hog. This is a second type of "distress" call and is used by hogs when severely threatened or wounded. Sometimes across a swamp you will hear one of these squeals and you can assume that a battle between hogs has taken place and a wound has been inflicted or threatened with enough vigor to be convincing! These are key times to get off your stand and begin to still hunt in the direction of the distress call.

- **AGGRESSION CALLS**

Before and during aggressive behavior, hogs will often use loud grunts and snorts as a warning of an imminent showdown. Like most barroom brawls, these fights usually begin with verbal threats. Females have been found by researchers to emit "low, strained groan-like grunts" but I have never heard one.

- **MATING CALLS**

Hogs make distinctive calls when preparing to mate. One researcher noted that females will stand erect and unmoving when the male mating call is used. One researcher even noted that domestic hogs stand so erect and at attention that they will allow a person to climb on their backs when this call is used. The boar hog makes a noise like an out-of-breath marathon runner. The female emits low grunt-like groans.

Scent Signals

The hog's strongest sense is his smell. It is also his strongest scent! You can smell a hog from quite a distance downwind if you know what you're sniffing for. I imagine hogs can detect the presence of other hogs at rather large distances. The hog's nose has been compared to the dog's and there are some scientists who believe the hog has the better snout!

Hogs distribute "musk" odor at times. This same musk scent has been detected in hog nests. There has been very little research in this area. Biologists have done some preliminary studies using hog estrus but there is much to be learned about this area of hog life. There is some indication that hogs use scent for mating purposes just like deer. Both deer and hogs are related as distant cousins (just think of the similarity in their tracks!) so this would not be shocking if found to be true.

A last mysterious thing about the "scent signals" of hogs is feces defecation sites. These areas have been noticed by different researchers and described to be areas where feces are deposited and are found in different stages of decomposition. These areas of droppings are found near an active hog trail and measure about 20 feet by 10 feet.

The purpose of these sites is unknown, but may be used like male dog urinating sites. If this is true, these areas may be some type of territorial marking, even though hogs tend to have overlapping territories with numerous family groups included.

Touch Signals

Hogs have two primary touch signals that they use with each other, grooming and rubbing. Grooming is done by sows to their young. The piglet stands at attention while mom licks the child, much like human mothers cleaning the face of a dirty kid! Piglets have been known to squirm and complain by saying, "Awe mom, quit!"

In domestic hogs, grooming is done between adults but I haven't met anyone who has documented this behavior in wild hogs although it would not surprise me if this were found to be true!

Rubbing is part of the mating ritual between a boar and a sow. The boar rubs the sexual regions (vulva) of the female to stimulate a desire to mate. This characteristic seems to be similar to a buck deer licking the genital areas of does to get them to stand for copulation. This mating ritual occurs when the sow is in estrus, the time when females are receptive to mating, because of ovulation and hormonal conditions.

General Hog Questions

Are hogs color blind?

Hogs are like no other animals. They have very poor eyesight, but they are not color blind. Scientists, using a machine called an Ultramicroelectrode, measure the nerve impulses between the eye and brain. From this information, they have concluded that the eyesight of hogs is very unique and is called "spectralvision." This means that hogs have very little ability to detect the differences between hues of colors. All objects appear to hogs as colored "blobs." Hogs cannot distinguish the contrasts between colors very well. This means that the boundaries between objects are not perceived as significant. In laymen's terms, a hog can see colors but cannot see a rainbow! A green-clad hunter appears as a bush (unless he is moving) and an orange-clad hunter probably appears as an orange nonthreatening blob! All objects appear as "flat planes of single colors."

Can you age hogs according to "tusk" length?

No, this is a common myth. Tusks grow the longest at about three years of age, when the hog is in his prime. They tend to be ground down as they eat and become shorter, not longer, as the hog gets old. Tusks also often break-off and regrow! Hogs with very long tusks generally have a dental problem. The tusks are misfitted and do not rub and scrape against the whetters as they are designed to do. This allows the tusks to grow to unusual lengths. Sows have tusks too, but they do not normally grow as long. Tusks are secondary sexual characteristics. Castration causes bars to have thicker tusks than most other boars.

How much do wild hogs generally weigh?

Mature wild hogs generally weigh around 150 pounds. Boars tend to be slightly larger than sows. Castrated wild boars sometimes reach in the upper 200's or low 300's. If fed and vaccinated for parasites, wild hogs can reach near 1,000 pounds, if they are also "short-term" wild hogs with a recent genetic link to domestics. Extremely large hogs are not normally "wild" in the truest sense of the word.

What are the "birthing" facts of hogs?

Researchers call the act of labor and delivery of piglets, farrowing. It takes between 45 minutes and 8 hours for a sow to "farrow" her young. The longer it takes a sow to farrow, the greater the mortality rates of the piglets. Sows generally farrow 4-8 piglets after a gestation period of approximately 115 days. There is a very high mortality rate, as much as 40%, in the birthing of piglets. Three main problems cause the suffocation of new piglets. The "membrane" that surrounds the piglet is sometimes broken in the act of labor and the piglet dies in the birth canal. Sometimes, after birth, the piglet is not able to escape from the membrane and the mother, unlike dogs and cats, does not eat the membrane from the young. Third, sows aren't always good mothers and kill their own young by laying on them. Sows also build short-term nests to have their piglets. Soon after birth, piglets need warmth and these nests provide this.

What are the stages of development of feral hogs?

There are many ways to classify hog development, but generally, from 0-7 weeks hogs are "juveniles" (unweaned). From 8-33 weeks they are "immature" (unable to breed). From 33-51 weeks they are "young adults" (possible but not likely to breed). After one year they are fully mature "adults."

How many males and females are present in a hog population?

The percentage of females and males in wild unhunted populations is probably close to 50/50, with a slight edge going to more males than females. The reason is that females have a higher mortality rate because of the increased danger of farrowing (giving birth).

Are hogs causing as much damage as is often reported?

There is some disagreement about this subject. Some biologists say that hogs have been here for more than 400 years and any great damage to the ecosystem has probably already occurred. Others say that hogs continue to be very devastating to native populations of plants and animals. Hogs destroy habitat. In the Great Smokey Mountains National Park in Tennessee, there has been a tremendous amount of destruction from hogs.

Hogs also damage a lot of private property. I was once invited to hog hunt from the roof of a house in an exclusive neighborhood because hogs were destroying the landscaping. Wild hogs do destroy roads and crops.

Since hogs are "exotics", they are considered a "pest" species. On private lands in Florida, they can be hunted year-round without limit. They also can be very destructive to agricultural crops.

There are many, many "exotic" species of plants and animals. They are not indigenous to our country. Other commonly recognized animals and plants that were imported to the United States include: Australian pine, kudzu, hydrilla, waterhyacinth, fire ants, blue tilapia, giant marine toad, Cuban treefrog, parakeets, muscovy ducks, and hundreds of others. Boa constrictors are even developing a "wild" population in the Miami, Florida area. In Texas and Arizona, the African honeybee has already begun to be established. The brown tree snake, highly poisonous, is poised and almost certain to be a new immigrant to our lands!

Why and how are hogs aggressive with each other?

Boars and sows have an absolute dominance social structure that begins when piglets fight to establish a suckling order with the sow. This dominance mode never changes in the hog. **Boars are aggressive as they seek mating dominance while females are aggressive to establish feeding privilege.**

Females tend to not use physical force when aggressive with other females and male aggression also tends to be mostly threat. Male aggressive behavior can become severe and result in the death of a boar although this is rare. Subordination is indicated when one hog turns and runs. The last pig standing is dominant!

Do boars and sows taste different?

Let me say this! If you shoot a boar, don't throw it away and assume that it won't be good eating. It is true that some boars are almost inedible, but almost all of the boars that the authors have shot have been fine eating. My first boar was pretty bad, but subsequent boars have been good! Out of all the many boars we have shot, only 3 have been bad and only a few have been distinguishable from the sows we've killed. The taste difference is probably over-rated in most cases.

Little Rooter learning wild hog habits from mom!

Mom teaching table manners at local water hole!

HOT DOGS

Stand Hunting Strategies

Favorite Stands, Blinds, and Scouting Methods

Chapter Five

- *What are the secrets to successful stand hunting?*
- *How do you scout for hogs and select a good stand site?*
- *What are the best kinds of stands to use in specific circumstances?*

Little Craig Weissinger was all of 11 years old when he shouldered his new shotgun for that predawn hike to his stand on his second hog hunt. On his first hunt, Craig had been overcome by "tusk" fever and missed his shot. This time he would be ready, he vowed. The second hog came from an unexpected direction just like the first. I turned my head and saw a 150 lb. sow approaching from the rear. She was lazily feeding and unaware of any impending danger. After getting little Craig turned and ready, I whispered for him to shoot. At the liftoff of the 20 gauge slug, 150 lbs. of black lightning decided that there were other places she preferred to be. We could hear the brush crashing as she exited the area. Craig was heartbroken. Two failed attempts at two nice hogs from the same stand.

The following week, little Craig couldn't make it, but one of my friends could. During the same "first hour" of morning that the two previous hogs had come past this stand, another one showed. At thirty yards, my friend Mike laid the crosshairs on the hog and fired. For the third time in three weeks, a hog charged off in fast retreat. A close examination proved that Mike's shot had been missed because of a pencil thin branch just a few feet in front of the gun. Three opportunities, three hogs, and no meat. Good strategies give you the "potential" of shooting game, but the rest is up to you!

Being at The Right Place at The Right Time

There are some important things to note from this story. *Good stand sites really produce.* Did you notice that three different hogs were seen from the same stand on three *consecutive* hunts? We were hunting on unbaited, heavily pressured public lands. A good stand location can really produce pork opportunities!

That is a common experience among my friends. We might sit quite a few mornings/evenings on unproductive stand sites before finding a good area. Once we find a hot area, we tend to see numerous pigs from the same stand. This occurs even if we have already shot hogs from this stand. Hogs are social animals, they will be found with others of their kind. What makes one hog like a particular area will make other hogs like that same area too!

Remember too that hogs are lazy. Your average wild pig is a workaholic compared to a common domestic pig, but he is still a creature that seeks the easiest way. He wants to find an area that has all his needs met within "armchair" distance. Once you find areas of recent activity, you know that you're close to his bedroom, living room, and kitchen too! That's why you shouldn't waste a lot of time hunting a stand where you seldom see pigs. Move to another spot! That's the proper way. In good hog territory, you'll find hog sign everywhere. As one outdoor writer has written, *"you can't eat sign."* Sign only tells you where the pig was yesterday or last week. Hunt pigs! And hunt for them until you find them. I normally commit to a stand site for at least three hunts before moving on to another site (I count morning and evening as two hunts). If I haven't seen a hog in that amount of time, I'm on to a different area (although some of these moves may only be a few hundred yards from the original site).

Another lesson of note is the great effectiveness of a tree stand. In each of our three hunts, the hog came to us and all we had to do was move carefully and shoot properly (something we failed to do). If you are a beginning hog hunter, trust us, find a good stand site, commit to it, and your chances of killing a hog have just skyrocketed! Stand hunting is the most effective way and the skills required are the easiest to acquire.

Basics of Stand Hunting

Stand hunting is sitting or standing in a *stationary* place, generally from a raised platform (but not always), and waiting for game to walk into your shooting zone. It is the "ambush" strategy of hunting and it has real advantages.

More hogs have probably been killed out of some type of raised stationary stand than all other methods put together. Think of the advantages of a raised stand. The average wild hog stands about 20-25 inches (including juvenile and adults) at the shoulder. That means that every low bush, fallen tree, and large mushroom is in his line of sight. He can't see very far because of his low height. A raised platform puts you out of his already limited line-of-sight. Remember too that hogs are widely recognized as having poor eyesight. When you put together the fact of his short height and his poor vision, it's easy to see how he can be very close and utterly unaware of your presence.

A stand is also an advantage because the hog's main defenses are his snout and ears. A stander's scent, if using a "raised" platform, is dispersed high above and helps hide your presence. A stand is also an advantage because you aren't moving as much as with other hunting strategies. Hogs quickly pick up movement, even with their bad sight. They also easily differentiate natural noises from unnatural ones. Broken sticks, shuffling leaves, and the sound of briars scraping against your clothing while walking are dead give-a-ways. Anytime you have to move, there is a danger of making an unexpected noise. A tree stand means there is less chance of making a wrong sound.

Of course, there are still plenty of wrong sounds that are characteristic of stands. Any metallic sound, such as that which might be caused by a gun barrel clinking or your stand creaking as you shift your weight, is enough to spook your hog. A lot of care needs to be made in "silencing" any stand that you use. If a pig decides it's time to move, it's normally too late to shoot, at least with any degree of accuracy. And yet, even with these characteristic dangers, a stand puts most of the odds in your favor, including the ease of shooting from a stable and rested position.

Types of Stands

The first question for you to decide is what kind of stand to use. I personally own all three different types of tree stands; a hang-on, a climber, and a ladder stand. I use each type of stand for different hunting situations. They all have distinct advantages and disadvantages.

- **Hang-On Stands**

Hang-on stands generally consist of a platform that chains or straps to the trunk of a tree. The hang-ons are lightweight (from

6 lbs. up), inexpensive (beginning around $60), and very portable. They are especially good for athletic, younger hunters. They are very helpful when hiking into remote areas or areas where a stand cannot be left behind.

There are two main problems with hang-ons. They tend to be uncomfortable when hunting long hours because they are small. Second, the access to the stand is limited to your system of climbing. Many hunters use tree steps which either screw into the tree itself or steps which strap to the tree and cause no harm. This is the primary method although tree sticks (similar to ladders which come in 3 and 4 foot sections) and tree climbers (spikes that are strapped to your boots) are also used. I prefer the screw-in tree steps when hunting private property although they are prohibited on most public land because of possible damage to the tree (please check your regulations). I use the hang-on stand primarily when I am hunting far from my truck or am moving around frequently trying to find the hogs. The portability is the main advantage. I can pack a hang-on stand and walk all day. This is an advantage that no other stand offers!

• Climbers

Climbers do just that, they are a stand that attaches to a tree and makes climbing easy. No tree steps or ladders are needed. Any tree of the proper diameter, without branches to the height you want to hunt, can be used. Climbers are nice because they are comfortable, stable, and generally larger than other stands. They begin around $150 and go up to about $300. They are a complete two-piece climbing system. Normally, one part is the seat and the other is the foot rest or platform. In some climbers, it is possible to stay in the tree for hours in comfort. There is plenty of room to stand and stretch. Some climbers enable you to take a nap, although this is rare.

The disadvantage to this type of stand is the number of pack mules necessary to get it into the woods. I'm kidding, but it is true that most climbers weigh about 20 lbs. or more (when compared to 10 lbs. for the average hang-on). This makes a hike into the woods to a previously chosen stand site fairly easy, but you can't scout with a climber strapped to your back.

My normal practice is to find my main hunting area using a hang-on. Once I've found an area where I want to spend time doing some serious hunting, I move in the climber and padlock it to a tree. I don't take my climber out of the woods each time I leave, even on most public lands. I'd rather hide it and risk losing it than pack it in each time (remember too, that I normally hunt deep and far away from most hunters). Climbers are more portable than ladder stands, but still have some bulk. If I had to use only one type of stand, I would choose a lighter-weight climber.

- **Ladder Stands**

Ladder stands are a good compromise between climbers and hang-ons. They are not nearly as portable as either, but they are inexpensive (near $100) and fairly roomy and comfortable. You don't have to be half monkey or Olympic gymnast to use one safely. Older and heavier hunters, or your child, will probably be more comfortable in a ladder stand. There is some danger in attaching the stand to a tree (we've all seen cartoons where a ladder is pushed off a wall), but a safe method of doing so should be part of the manufacturer's instructions.

There is not a whole lot of variety when it comes to your basic ladder stand. All ladder stands consist of a ladder, a platform, and some method of tying the stand to the tree. The major differences from one manufacturer to another are weight and expandability. Some ladder stands are sectioned and can be backpacked in three of four foot pieces while others must be dragged while fully extended. Height can be added to some ladder stands by buying an extension.

Good stand location produces opportunity!

There are two specialty ladder-type stands worthy of mention. The first is a stand that allows TWO hunters to hunt together. These are usually ladder stands with *two* seats positioned one right above the other. I use this stand to take my kid along. This is one of the only stands on the market today which allows direct supervision and contact to be maintained with a young hunter. Another special occasion stand is the Texas Tripod type stands which are free standing (no tree needed to attach it to) and often used in fields or when there are no close suitable trees. This kind of stand would be great to use over many Florida palmetto fields.

• Ground Blinds

A last kind of stand is the most natural, inexpensive, and simple. Find a good tree in the right spot and take a seat. I've killed just as many big-game animals sitting by a tree as I have hiding in the heights. A manufactured tree seat will enable you to sit at ground level and be comfortable. The big advantage of sitting at the base of a tree is there is absolutely no noise in setup. When I'm hunting an area where I haven't yet picked a stand site, I often sneak in and find a tree in the dark and setup a seat.

Ground blinds can also be used. Manufactured ones run between $15-$100. A camouflage piece of burlap can also be used. It can be clipped or tied to the bushes around you. Your view and scent distribution are not as good as from a raised platform, but there are times when a simple entry makes good hunting sense.

How do most fatal accidents happen?

One last warning about tree stands. I've worked with the Hunter's Education programs of various states. Each year I receive the accident statistics. Most people think that the majority of hunting accidents occur when someone gets shot because some idiot thought they were a deer or hog. These "*mistaken for game*" shootings are actually somewhat rare when compared to tree stand accidents. Fatal accidents are common from just a few feet off the ground. Wear a safety belt even while climbing. It could just save you from a broken ankle or something far worse!

SCOUTING A STAND SITE

Hogs, like most big-game animals, are "edge" creatures. They live in more than one kind of habitat area and spend their lives walking from one to another. Scientific studies indicate that *"variety"* of habitat is an important hog consideration. In other words, if an area has nothing but great acorn trees, it probably isn't a great hog area, even though hogs love acorns when in season. Hogs need cover, water, safety, and food. Acorns make up only one part of their diet. If an area has nothing but acorns, what will the pigs eat after the acorn crop is gone? Variety in habitat is important.

This helps us know where to look for a stand site. I have often placed good stands in the middle of swamps, palmetto fields, cypress heads, slash pine areas, as well as pastures and oak heads. *These single habitat stands are great at times, but I prefer finding a stand site which looks into at least two, rather than one, of these different kinds of habitat.*

In the hog story at the beginning of this chapter, little Craig and I were located at the edge of a swamp, overlooking an oak head in front of us, with a palmetto field to our left. We could literally have shot a hog standing in water, or in 30 inch high palmetto's, or eating acorns! All from the same tree stand! Generally these "edges" are the preferred stand sites although there are many times when I break that rule because the "signs" of hog presence is just too clear!

Stand hunting is deceptive. There is a lot of work needed to be successful. The first job is to find the right area. Scouting cannot be overemphasized. The reason that most people don't kill hogs is that they are poor scouts! You can have the nicest stand, located at the perfect height, and sit there until hell freezes over and never see a hog. *Your skill at finding hog territory is the number one priority to concentrate on.*

You need to learn the difference between week old sign and day old sign. You need to see and think like a pig (your wife might testify that you can already do that). *If you don't have time to scout, then "stand-hunting" is not the type of hunting you should be doing.* There are other hunting methods that require far less prior work (and are generally less successful). If you are new to a hunting area and don't yet have a good mental picture of the area, stand hunting is a hit or miss adventure.

Here are the questions to ask as you scout for a stand site. *What evidence is there that hogs frequent this area? Why would a hog want to walk through this area? What is here to draw him? Is this a rooting area, or are acorns dropping, or is this thick area the perfect place for him to hide during the day?* Answer these questions correctly and the battle is mostly done.

In one of my favorite areas, I have numerous stand sites between a swamp and palmetto field. The hogs travel from one to the other. Mature oaks circle the field. The pigs can rest and hide in the palmetto's, wallow in the swamp, and feed on the acorns. My friend Scott was sitting on one of these stands this past hunting season. He was sitting in the middle of a palmetto field in his ladder stand. He heard hogs crashing through the field as they neared him. This experienced hunter slowly stood and began searching for a shot. The hogs came single file past him, but he could never find one to shoot. For over an hour, as one hog exited the field, another entered it. Because the hogs were shorter than the palmetto's, one had to come right past him to offer a shot. Scott believes that at least 12 hogs walked past him that evening and none made a fatal error. Another hunter and I were just a few hundred yards away and never saw a pig. Scouting makes a difference!

The most important thing to do on the stand - STAY THERE!

The most difficult part of stand hunting is sitting at attention for hours on end. Most struggling hunters give up too soon on the stand and begin to walk the woods. When you are sitting there for hours, it's easy to think that a whole herd of swine is located just out of sight. The temptation often becomes too much for the unsuccessful hunter and out of the tree he comes. Let me make a point that is worth the price of this book. *If you don't have the patience to sit in a tree stand, you surely don't have the patience needed to still hunt successfully.*

I know that it's difficult to stay in your stand for hours. Please understand that it's much more difficult to move and stumble across an unsuspecting hog that will allow you a good shot. In other words, if you aren't yet what could be called a "successful" hog hunter, force yourself to stay in the tree. Don't kid yourself that you will kill hogs by walking around. If you do happen to get down and walk up on a hog and kill it, I'm afraid that you will probably never be a decent hunter. That stroke of luck will curse

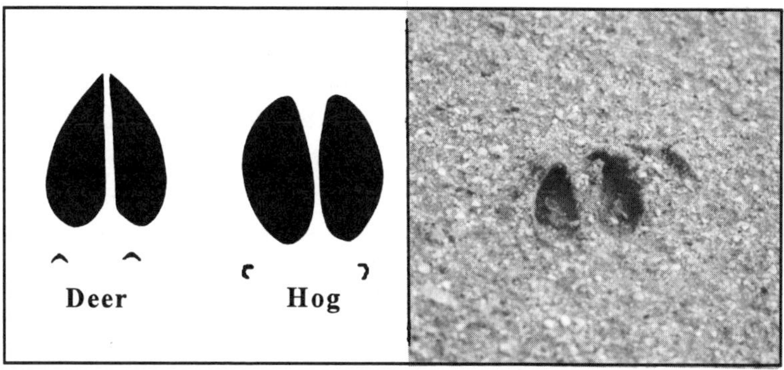

Hog hooves are more rounded and digits are generally separated!

you for years to come. Years from now, you will be telling your grandchildren of that special hunt, back in the 20th century, when you killed your one and only hog. Do you get the hint that I really think you should "commit" to a stand to be a successful hunter? The top hours to be alert in your stand are the first three hours and the last three hours of the day. About 80% of the hogs we kill are killed during this time, especially on public lands. The more hunting pressure placed on a property, the earlier and later hogs will tend to move. To test this theory, keep a record of the number of shots you hear on a hunt. Those statistics will prove us right!

What to do as the hog approaches.

You hear him coming through the swamp, or maybe through the leaves under the oaks. You thought you heard something a minute ago, but now you're sure. The first thing to do is slowly move your barrel so that it is pointed in the general direction of the sound. Don't shoulder or aim in that direction yet, just have the gun pointed high in that area. The reason is simple, there are a lot of people and other animals that make a lot of racket. If you are hog hunting, you tend to assume that each approaching noise is a hog. If you are deer hunting, that same sound becomes a deer. This human tendency is what gets people killed. If you have your gun pointed in the general direction of the approaching sound, this should be plenty of preparation.

The next thing for you to do is keep both eyes open and begin looking for movement and color. Don't look for a whole hog, but a piece of a hog. Hogs are mostly black in color although we have a lot of brown (red) ones. White spots or speckles on these are also common. When you finally see the hog, immediately look ahead of him in the direction he is going. Find an open area that he is likely to walk through. These open areas become your shooting lanes. When the hog lowers his head, turns away from you, or goes behind an obstruction, slowly shoulder your gun and aim generally at him. Follow him as he approaches one of the shooting lanes. If there is only one good shooting lane available, you have to stop him when he gets there. Say "hello" to him or "hey". That is usually enough to get him to stop and look in your direction. Now there are different theories on where to shoot a hog. It all depends on your marksmanship skills and experience. If you are

What do you do when a hog approaches? Shoot it!

nervous and somewhat unsure of yourself, aim just behind the front shoulder nearest you when he turns broadside and let him have it. He's likely to run, but if hit in the right area will not go more than 100 yards.

All big-game animals have their organs split into two areas inside the body cavity. The heart and lungs are located just forward of the mid-point of the animal and extend past the front shoulders. The intestines, liver, stomach, and other organs are located in the back half of the animal. These two sections are separated by a layer of elastic-like material called a diaphragm. This is important

You can't beat the comfort of a permanant stand!

You can't beat the flexibility of a portable stand!

to know because we always want to shoot hogs in the forward compartment that holds the heart and lungs. Death comes from massive blood loss, collapse of lungs, suffocation, and a damaged heart that cannot pump blood. Animals hit in this area are generally dead within 30 seconds. But in 30 seconds, these animals can travel a great distance.

If you are experienced, a shot below the ear is my favorite spot. I say you must be experienced because only experience will help you determine if the circumstances are stable enough to provide a good chance at success. Hogs don't move their heads nearly as much as deer so a head shot can be a fairly easy maneuver. I like the head shot because trailing becomes unnecessary and damage to meat is nonexistent. I also am aware of many, many hunters who can't seem to put a bullet where they are aiming. If you've missed or wounded a hog or two, take the sure shot and go for the heart/lung area. I only take a head shot when the hog is within 50 yards and is stopping to feed in open areas. If a hog is moving or is in any kind of cover, I take the shoulder shot.

After the shot there are a couple of very important principles to remember. The first is this, "<u>mark the spots in your mind where you shot him and where you last saw him</u>." Say out loud, to yourself, the details of those two important spots. This helps you not to forget them. I usually say something like this, "*OK, he was stopped just past that ditch and a little left of that stump and I last saw him in that opening by the big oak tree.*"

If you don't say such things, you will be amazed at how difficult it can be to find where he was standing and where he went. Your perspective from the tree will be difficult to see from the ground. Mark him well before you move off your stand!

You must also realize that many well-hit animals run off as if they were never touched. You can't tell if you hit a hog by how he runs (although squeals are generally a good indicator). Most new hunters don't realize that television has ruined their hunting. On TV, when anyone is shot, they fall down and die. This does not normally happen in real life. A well-shot big-game animal can travel more than 100 yards with no functioning heart or lungs.

In other words, beginner hunters tend to doubt their shot *("I've missed before"* syndrome) and therefore don't search adequately to find the hog they've killed. I'm just arrogant enough to believe I can't miss so I assume that every hog I shoot is dead. You probably don't think that way and will give up too soon. Let me warn you, it's a heartbreaking thing to come into the woods the next day or the next week and find a hog carcass just 75 yards from where you supposedly missed. I told you before that you can't eat sign, but you also can't eat carrion.

Are hogs as aggressive as you have heard? Hog attack stories are exaggerated. Hogs generally run at first sight of you like any other wild animal. If you are going to be charged, approaching a wounded hog is probably where it will happen. Stay in your stand a good half-hour before beginning the track. Unless it is raining, there is no advantage to leaving right away. Spend that half-hour or so searching for the spot where you shot him and trying to find some blood within sight of your stand.

I like to carry toilet paper to mark the spots where I find blood. I leave a small sheet to mark each spot. That way, if I lose the trail, or if he doubles back on his trail, I can easily find it. It also helps slow me down and relax me as I go.Look for the next blood spot before moving from the one you are standing over. Slowly and carefully follow him. Remember to have your gun reloaded and ready to go, but keep the safety on. The authors have never had a hog charge us and don't think it likely. Also, it's important to remember that blood can be left on branches and leaves at shoulder height as he runs through the woods.

When you find your hog, approach carefully. The tusks on the males are razor sharp and can cut through your jeans or clothes like a hot knife through butter. Watch the hog for a minute from a distance before approaching. Poke the hog from the rear and then put your barrel into his eye. *If he doesn't blink or rip your leg off, he's probably dead and safe to handle.* Also be aware that the tusks can still cut after he's dead. When you handle his head, use the same care that you would use when handling a razor-sharp knife.

A REVIEW OF THE MAIN PRINCIPLES OF SUCCESSFUL STAND HUNTING

Take it from the experts, make the following commitments and your stand hunting will be successful.

√ Commit to the needed time for good scouting.
√ Find a number of different stand sites in high concentration areas.
√ Stay in your stand for at least three hunting periods before moving.
√ Change what isn't working until you find success.
√ Movements in the stand must be slow, deliberate, and well-timed.
√ The higher the stand, the less likely you are to be seen or scented.
√ After the shot, mark the spots, in your mind, where you shot at the hog and where you last saw him.
√ Approach a dead hog as if he were only wounded because "dead" hogs sometimes bite.

MY WIFE SAYS IT'S UGLY AND I HAVE TO HANG IT IN THE GARAGE...
SOW'S... CAN'T LIVE WITH 'EM, CAN'T LIVE WITHOUT 'EM.

Still Hunting Strategies

A REAL CHALLENGE FOR THE EXPERIENCED HUNTER!

Chapter Six

- What conditions make the best "still hunting" opportunities?
- What do you do if a hog sees you or senses danger?
- What are the basic principles to keep in mind when still hunting?

I had been moving very slowly for almost an hour. Earlier that morning I heard one prolonged squeal from my stand and knew at least one porker was on the other side of the creek fighting with a brother or sister. I got down from my stand, crossed the creek, and began my "still hunt" through the bottom land.

I had been standing in the same spot for about 5 minutes, body still, eyes working overtime. I sensed that something was close. I looked through the brush for some sign, some sound, some movement. And then I heard a muffled grunt. About 50 yards in front of me was high grass, the kind that you see in marsh areas. As I stood there wondering if a hog could be in that high grass, one stepped out and immediately back into the grass. I began to see numerous areas where it looked like the grass was being moved by feeding hogs.

One step at a time, carefully feeling the ground beneath my boots before placing my full weight down, I made my way over to the sea of grass. When I reached the edge, I heard one hog chase another for a few steps. They were in there all right! I slowly entered the grass with them. When they moved or squealed or grunted, I moved. After 5 minutes, I was only 20 steps into the grass, but just then I saw the grass parting and a hog approaching. I shouldered my rifle just as the porker appeared a scant 8 yards in front of me. A quick shot and the sea of grass exploded with hogs in mass retreat! After my heart stopped blasting out of my chest, I dragged her out. My hog was a 125 lb. female, the perfect eating-size sow!

Who Should Still Hunt?

In the last chapter, I assumed that you were somewhat new to hunting and new to hogs in particular. In this chapter, I am going to make the opposite assumption. I am going to assume that you have become quite skilled at stand hunting and are ready for a new challenge. You have a number of hogs under your belt and you're ready for the next level. Your success rate will probably be lower than with stand hunting, but each hog killed will be a greater accomplishment.

Still Hunting Basics

Still hunting refers to the strategy of moving slowly through the woods, so slowly it might seem that you are "standing still." The object of stand hunting is waiting for hogs to walk past you. The object of still hunting is spotting game before it spots you. Whereas stand hunting is the *ambush* or *sniper* method of hunting, still hunting is the *search and destroy* method.

Still hunting, like no other strategy, puts your skills, knowledge, and patience against those of your quarry. Hogs are intelligent animals and they quickly figure out that hunters are dangerous. Your average hog has seen his friends and family fall down and die when the human with the loud "thunder" stick is near. If you kill a hog still hunting, you have truly matched your skills against his and vanquished the foe!

4 Rules of Still Hunting

Rule One - Know Thyself

The first rule of still hunting is to know yourself. I mean by this thait is important for you to understand your own impatience and characteristic mistakes. The number one mistake of still hunting is speed. You, the hunter, are preoccupied with looking for hogs. Your tendency is to watch the horizon and move quickly through the area before you. That is the characteristic mistake of most still hunters.

As I've previously pointed out, hogs are short animals. They are easily obstructed by anything and everything. While still hunting, you must spot him first. This means that slow and careful is the name of the game, even when you think you clearly see that no hog is near. You must assume that hogs are close, even when you see they are not. Almost always when I encounter an animal, I am amazed at how close I've gotten before I spotted him. It's as if game animals appear out of nowhere. Don't trust your eyes - always assume that a hog is within shooting distance.

Excellent still hunting area. Oak trees loaded with acorns.

There is another reason for a slow pace. Hogs spot movement! The faster you move in contrast to the swaying trees around you, the easier it is for a pig to spot you. Be as the tree, still hunter, and sway with the wind. This means one half-step at a time, rather than eight or ten steps in rapid succession. There are times when I will take as many as 4 steps without stopping, but that is when I am really flying.

Here is the test. In a few hour's walk you will only cover a few hundred yards. You will only be a few hundred yards from your truck, or from where you left your friend, or from the stand that you sat in all morning without seeing a hog. That's why still hunting is so very difficult. You've only covered a limited amount of land in a long period of time. *If you can be satisfied with that, you can be a still hunter.* If that will frustrate you and cause you to want to cover more and more territory, you don't have the patience for this strategy.

Discipline is the key word! It takes extreme discipline on your part to move slowly through the forest. You must be sure and convinced. Convinced that hogs are indeed using this specific area. Convinced also that the pig is somewhere very near. He is lying there napping behind that next fallen tree or slowly feeding along that brushy area. If you have the mind-set that he is somewhere else, you'll never be a successful still hunter, because you will be in a rush to get there!

I like to think this way, "*It's only a matter of time before I see a hog.*" If I walk slowly through hog territory, I am bound, sooner or later, to walk up on a hog or group of hogs. It may not happen today, but it will happen. As a matter of fact, wildlife biologists use a very similar method to still hunting to determine the number of game animals in an area. They count how many animals they jump in a certain amount of time of walking through the woods. They place this number in a scientific calculation and by this get a fairly accurate estimate of game populations.

The real question, therefore, is not if you will encounter a pig. The important question is this, "*What will be the circumstances when it happens?*"

- *Will I be making so much noise that the hogs exit the area before I even know they are there?*
- *Will it be at a time when I am seen before I see?*
- *Or will it be when I am ready for the encounter and the hog is unaware?*

Those choices are really up to you. You will encounter hogs. You will also choose the circumstances of the encounter. Your speed and carefulness will determine the success of the encounter!

Rule Two - Know Thy Prey

The forest, the swamp, and the field are the home of the hog. Think of how slowly and relaxed you move around in the midst of your home. Think of the average trip to the refrigerator. You sit by the TV and wait until you get a desire for a snack. You stand, pat the dog on the head and begin the trip. A headline from the paper catches your eye and you pause before deciding to read it later. The kids yell from the next room and you stop to determine if they are fighting or playing. Finally, after all these stops and starts, you reach the refrigerator.

My point is simple. In your home, you are not in a hurry to do anything! You live there and are relaxed and nonchalant about your movements. The hog is no different. *He isn't in a great hurry to get anywhere.* When the hunter enters his territory, he is entering an alien place. We don't see the same things the animals see. We aren't drawn to the same plants, the same places, the same sounds, and aren't even aware of the scents they smell. Yet the main difference is this, the pig doesn't have anywhere to go, but the hunter is in a hurry. That is the hog's main advantage. It's really a psychological advantage. If you were studying tree bark or counting acorns, you would see more hogs because your pace would be different.

The hog has his characteristic faults too. He grunts to keep in touch with other hogs, squeals when he fights, makes noises when eating, and walks not too quietly in the woods. His eyesight is very poor and he is not as wary as other big-game animals. All of these facts make still hunting hogs a potential success!

What are we looking for when we are slowly moving through the forest? *The first thing to realize is that you are NOT looking for a whole hog!* You are looking for a piece of a hog. An ear, a leg, or a splotch of color that is out-of-place, these are the things to watch for! I like to watch for "*horizontal lines.*" Horizontal lines are somewhat rare in nature, but the back of a hog is horizontal. I also watch for movement. This, more than anything, is what I see most often. I also realize that when I am moving, I cannot see something else moving!

Binoculars are a real advantage in still hunting. *I don't often use them to see long distances, but instead to see through brush and into thick areas where the naked eye cannot.* Binoculars allow you to have Superman x-ray vision! It works this way. Your eyes focus on the nearest bushes or brush when looking into a thick area. A binocular allows you to change the focus and see deeper into an area. As you change the focus on your binocular, you are changing the distance of the focus area. You will be amazed at how effectively this little trick works!

Hogs can even be still hunted in open fields if carefully approached. I got within 40 yards of these wild hogs with my camara.

Rule Three - Know Thy Path

There are a few key considerations that will determine the success of your still hunting.

- ***Since you are moving so slowly, you must choose your route carefully!***

People who hunt with me are sometimes amazed at the morning's hunt! I will walk almost as fast as I can for miles - so much so that many times my "beginning hunters" are almost exhausted - then, for no apparent reason, my pace will slow to a snail's pace. The reason is simple, there is no need to go slow in bad hog territory. I will almost race to the area that I plan to still hunt - but once there - every step is planned and careful! Scouting determines *"high-concentration areas"* where still hunting is likely to be successful.

The moment of truth!

- ***You must feel the ground with your feet to remain quiet!***

Many branches and "noise-making" vegetation are located where you can't see it. Slowly putting your foot down, and slowly adding weight to that foot, will make each step much more quiet. Don't be so committed to a straight line route that you walk through noisy areas, take a detour. Remember, the goal is not to travel long distances but to spot hogs!

- ***You must move with the wind in your favor!***

We rely on sight. Hogs rely on scent! They can therefore "see" you with their nose, even when they are located in thick bedding areas or over the next hill! If the wind is in your face or quartering from the side, you are going in the right direction!

- ***Don't forget to watch your sides and behind you!***

Hogs are very likely to walk up on you while you are "ghosting" through the woods. Keep a good lookout all around you while you are hunting.

- ***You must travel at the proper pace!***

The secret is to sound like another wild animal. Wild animals seldom keep a "constant" pace. They take a few steps, stop, pause, then take a single step, then five or six steps. This is the kind of "erratic pace" that you should aim to copy!

- ***You must know what to do when you make an unnatural noise!***

Be still, be quiet, and watch all around you! When wild animals hear an unnatural noise, they go through a predictable pattern. They stop, turn their heads in the direction of the noise, and wait. If the noise is close, this pause may be for several minutes, but generally, for only a solid minute or so! After this pause, they will often drop their heads as to feed and again go into a listening phase. Another common part of this ritual is to move slightly while still paying attention. If the animal senses no danger, it will go back to natural activity and act like it never heard anything at all! If the animal senses danger, it will turn and travel slowly away. Only if an animal "spots" you will it make a hasty retreat!

Rule Four - Know Thy Stalk

Still hunting is "looking" for hogs. Stalking is the act of approaching closer to an animal after you have spotted it. Still hunting is a skill, stalking is an art form! Watch any television nature show and you will see masters of the art - leopards and lions and cheetahs. The secret is to move without being noticed. Here are the secrets and tips for success!

- Move when the hog moves or lowers it's head.
- Move silently - don't watch the hog so much that you don't look down to see what path you are taking.
- Move behind trees or obstacles that will prevent the hog from seeing you. Use these obstacles to move closer and don't worry about keeping an eye on the hog the whole time you are moving.
- Move until you are within good shooting range and then find a good rest. My favorite rest is a kneeling position beside the trunk of a tree, although I probably use the sitting position more often because when the time is right, it's time to shoot!
- If a hog stops and looks and I see it pausing, I try to determine a few things. If the wind is in my favor - I will freeze and not move at all. I may lose the hog, but often, even if spooked, it will only "walk" away and I may get my shot. If the wind is not in my favor, I will slowly shoulder my rifle, even as the hog watches me. I will speed up the process only if the porker starts to run.

- If the hog begins to run, I often get into shooting position and wait. Rather than risk a running shot, I know that the hog will sometimes pause and look back. I want to be ready and waiting when that happens. This means that I sometimes don't take a shot, but it also means that I don't wound many hogs.
- If I spook a hog, I sometimes grunt or fake a squeal to see if I can get him to pause for a moment. Do this after shouldering your rifle; there's nothing worse than succeeding in stopping a running animal only to be unprepared to cash-in on the opportunity.
- If the hog runs, I like to circle and cut him off. One of my first hogs was killed in this way. The hog will probably only run a few hundred yards before slowing to a walk. If I ever run while hunting, this is the time. I run at an angle right or left of where the hog ran. I run for about a hundred yards and then walk quickly. Many times I've caught a hog turning to gain my scent!

Typical hog rooting in good still hunting areas.

The kick is a bit much, but the penetration is excellent!!

SPECIAL WEAPONS HUNTING

Shotguns, Bows, Muzzleloaders and Pistols

Chapter Seven

- How is a big boar's body different from a sow's?
- Why are pure or hybrid Russian Boar harder to kill than pure Feral Hogs?
- What "accessory" would greatly improve hog recovery after the shot with all special weapons?

Wade sat at the edge of the Oak Hammock waiting for his first hog! We had placed him on this stand because hogs were obviously coming out of the swamps, through a small palmetto field, and into this head to feed. This was a high acorn-yield year and the surrounding hardwood sections were under water. Wade's spot was the only high ground in our area with acorns. You could hear hogs splashing through the surrounding swamp as they approached.

With adrenaline pumping, Wade stood up and began looking for the hog! He heard the porker enter the palmetto field. A few steps, long moments of silence, followed by another step or two - but sure enough - he was coming! At 40 yards Wade saw his first glimpse of red razorback. He raised his shotgun and waited. At thirty yards the 160 pound boar came into an opening and turned broadside. Wade squeezed off his first shot.

The squeal dance began! From our stands we heard the first shot, a squeal, a second shot, another squeal, a third shot, a squeal, and a fourth shot - then silence! We were sure of two things. First - the hog was hit! Second, Wade would forever be teased about "machine gun hunting" for hogs.

Since it was his first hog we got down and went over to congratulate him and "rib" him a little. The biggest surprise came when we opened up the hog! NONE OF THE BUCKSHOT HAD ENTERED THE HOG BUT HAD STOPPED IN THE HIDE! Wade had loaded a buckshot, followed by a slug, then another load of buckshot, and finally another slug. The two slugs had done the dirty deed - but the buckshot had failed!

Why a Chapter on "Special Weapons"?

My friends and I have lost quite a few hogs because we underestimated the difficulty of bringing down this big-game animal. A few words to the wise may save you a difficult search for an animal that has not been adequately hit.

All big-game animals can travel amazing distances when hit properly with more than adequate weapons. I am not against shooting hogs with special weapons, but care must be taken to understand the extent of the challenge.

Thick Skinned Game

It is true that any cartridge or weapon that is adequate for deer will also be adequate for hogs, but there are some differences and hints that will make your hunting more successful.

Hogs are a tough, thick-skinned animals. Their hide is harder and thicker than deer. The skin of boars especially is different and Eurasian or Hybrids even more so. The shield covers the heart-lung area when a hog is broadside, and sometimes runs down the whole side of the animal. Hybrids and Russian Boar tend to have even thicker "shields" than pure Feral hogs. On a guided hunt, I was able to touch the shields on a large, captured Hybrid boar. *The shields were more than 2 inches thick and as hard as plywood.* These shields are like "bullet proof" vests for hogs.

This special weapons hog travelled only 20 yards after being hit!

This should be a special consideration to buckshot hunters, pistol shooters, and muzzleloaders. All three of these weapons shoot a fairly slow projectile that will have some difficulty in penetrating the shield, especially at the longer ranges of these weapons. Close shots are the secret to success with buckshot, pistols, and muzzleloaders. The solution is to make sure that the animal is "I can smell the musk scent" near.

Even rifle hunters need to be aware of the thick shields. Bullet selection and bullet weight need to be on the "upper" levels of most weapons. One guide told me the story of a client who brought a wildcat magnum rifle out to hunt his hybrid trophy boars. At 150 yards, in the middle of an improved pasture, the client shot the boar. The big hog lay down, got up and began staggering around as if drunk. The $2,400 gun sent out it's second missile. This time the boar fell down and began to groan. A third shot did not finish the hog off. The guide approached and shot the boar in the head with a handgun to put the poor pig out of his misery. When they skinned-out the hog, they were shocked to find that the magnum 165 grain bullet had not entered the body cavity. The lungs of the boar had collapsed from the energy of impact, but the bullet had not penetrated. It had "pushed" the hog to death!

Bullets expand at different rates depending upon their design. If you are shooting an "eater sow", any deer bullet will suffice, but if you are after trophy boar, choose a bullet designed for "thick-skinned" animals. Don't be fooled by the "department store clerk" who claims that this is ridiculous. Take the "know-it-all" looks of disbelief from the clerk and be prepared if you are truly going after trophy boar!

Surprisingly, bow-hunters will probably not have any problem penetrating shields. Sharp arrows from bows with good draw weights should cut right through. If you shoot a marginal draw weight bow (less than 50 pounds) you might be in some trouble. I like shooting carbon arrows and find that these penetrate just as effectively as heavier aluminum arrows. Shorter arrows from overdraws will also work, but again, close is the name of the game.

Difficult Recovery

Well-hit animals with any special weapon will act no differently than well-hit animals shot with rifles. I've knocked hogs down in their tracks with a bow and arrow! Animals hit in the center of the vitals, forward of the diaphragm, will go down in 100 yards or less. The problem occurs in animals that are not perfectly hit!

If the shot has been marginal, hogs are especially tough to recover. They tend to bleed less than deer. I believe this is caused by the thick skin and seasonal fat layer underneath. Hogs seem to "seal up" faster than deer and other big-game animals. Their habitat is generally wetter than deer habitat, thus adding to the difficulty of tracking.

For bow-hunters, I highly recommend a "tracker" system. This is a thin line, like kite string, which is attached to the arrow. When the hog runs, the string zips from the bow and follows the animal. You then follow the string. If you lose the hog, and he dies hundreds of yards from you, he can be found by finding the trailing line. This line also will indicate whether the hog is down (line not moving) or still traveling (line moving). If the line is moving, don't push the animal but stay back and let him stop and die! In my experience, the "tracker" system doesn't significantly affect arrow accuracy or speed out to about 30 yards - and this is the limit anyway with thick-skinned game!

There is an "accessory" that would make the committed special weapon's hunter a much greater success. You should strongly consider training a "trail dog" to recover poorly hit animals. Trail dogs do not fight hogs and are used only to find the wounded animal. See the chapter on "dog hunting" to learn the basics of training trail dogs.

CAN YOU GUARANTEE A 200 POUND RED NECK ??!!
WE GUARANTEE THE OPPORTUNITY FOR $400, BUT THE SHOOTINGS UP TO YOU.

Guided Wild Hog Hunting

Chapter Eight

- What is a typical guided hunt like?
- What are the possible options that can be chosen?
- What are the two types of guided hunts available?
- What questions should I ask to shop for a good guided hunt?

Jack, owner of Wild Hog Trophies, picked me up at the Walmart parking lot just as he promised. We arrived at the ranch house at 5:00 a.m. and breakfast was already cooking. There were two other hunters in camp for the day and Jack's son was guiding them. They were planning on gun hunting from stands. I was here to bow hunt trophy boar! After breakfast, we each said "good luck" and headed out to hunt.

We exited the truck just as the sun was starting to rise over the horizon and headed into a swamp bottom. He instructed me to keep my eyes on the horizon and to watch the creek to my right for any movement.

We hadn't walked far when we saw a hog coming toward us. Jack slowly moved me behind a tree as we waited to see what was coming. At 80 yards we could see that it was a 200+ boar with 3 inch visible tusks. Jack whispered to me that his part was over and it was all up to me! I quickly saw that the boar was going to pass us at too far a distance for a good shot. When he went behind a big oak, I ghosted to my right about 10 yards. I did this twice more and was in position. The boar came on as if he didn't have a thing to worry about in the world. At 30 yards I drew, at 25 I released. With a great huff the boar turned and ran. I looked back at Jack who gave me the thumbs up. We found him 30 minutes later!

The Advantages of Guided Hunting

Guided hunts take place where game is present and the expert is near! All the prior work of land access and scouting has already been done. After the kill, guides will field dress your hog and either butcher it or have a processor available who will. A good guide is also a teacher. He will be able to show you why hogs are present in a certain area and this will help you know how to better hunt them on your own. As a matter of fact, I think this is the primary reason to use a guide, to learn first-hand from an expert! Even after the kill, ask questions and have the guide show you what he sees.

Guided hunts can also save you time and money. They come in all kinds of price ranges, but most are in the $300-600 range. They save you time and money because multiple failed attempts on your own will be expensive. All hunting is fairly expensive, if you calculate the per pound of meat cost. For example, if I spend $75 a hunt and it takes me 6 hunts to kill a hog, I've spent $450 and 50-60 hours of time. When compared to a $400 guided hunt and 6 hours invested, you can see the savings!

What are the options in guided hunts?

Guided hunts are like cars, you can buy an inexpensive but reliable one or you can get one with all the bells and whistles. If you have a business associate who hunts, there is nothing more impressive and fun than to go to a place that has a dining room, shooting range, fishing ponds, and overnight facilities. A hog hunt can include other very fun activities. If you are on a shoestring budget and want a good hunt, this is possible with a good guide who has nothing but access to private land and a truck! The hunting is the same. The exteriors are what make the difference.

There are other options that must be considered. Guides tend to specialize in certain strategies for hog hunting. Some guides cater to bow-hunters exclusively. Others use dogs. As a matter of fact, if you have always wanted to go "dog hunting" for hogs, a guided dog hunt might be the ticket! There are two main types of guided hunts - preserve and private lease hunting.

Preserve Hunting

Preserves are fenced areas where the owner "owns" the game because he has bought and paid for them and placed them within his boundaries. All native wild game in the United States belongs to the people and not to the landowner, except on a preserve. If a man owns a 50,000 acre ranch, every deer, duck and quail on his property does NOT belong to him. That's why all hunting regulations, including limits and seasons apply to private land owners despite the amount of land that they own. This is true of all game except wild hogs. Because wild hogs are considered a "pest" species on private property, the landowner "owns" the hogs on his property (because they are non-native).

Great 200 pound boar from a quality guided hunt!

A preserve owner has sectioned off part of his land and placed his own animals in it. For a preserve offering deer hunting, this means that there must be a fence in place, but for hogs this is not necessary. The preserve owner who has hogs available either traps the hogs himself from another section of land or buys them from a professional trapper. Since preserve owners own all the game, there are no license fees (some states require a "preserve" license which is different from a regular hunting license), no limits (except how much you want to pay), and in most states year-long seasons (although with hogs, this is never an issue on private land).

When you think of a "fenced" area, don't think that the hunting will necessarily be easy. Put a few wild hogs in a 50 acre fenced area and you will have one heck of a time finding them.

Preserves have the advantage of knowing exactly what animals you will have the opportunity of shooting. If you call a preserve and tell them that you want to hunt a 200-pound black boar, it can be arranged! The disadvantage of preserve hunting is that it can be too "canned" for my tastes. Poorly run preserves take all the adventure and mystery out of the hunt by making it too easy! A good preserve gives a good hunt and that, to me, is what is important. Fair-chase rules should apply that will allow the hog to have a fighting chance to live and escape being killed!

Private Lease Hunts

Private lease hunts normally offer much greater land areas than preserves. It is truly "wild" hunting, but guides here too have their own tricks to insure success. Many guides have feeders placed throughout the property with timers set for release at specific times. In this way, there is some predictability of when hogs will be in certain areas. If the morning's hunt has gone poorly, a good guide will have a noon feeder set to go and guide you in that direction so the hunt won't be a failure. Some leases are so full of hogs that this is totally unnecessary. I took some of the pictures for this book on a private lease where I was told that every evening I would see between 30 and 300 hogs. The guide was right, in two hours I saw more than 200 hogs! Now that's a game rich environment and the kind of hunting that private leases can sometimes provide.

How to Shop for a Guided Hunt!

1. Set Your Own Goal

When you call to talk with a guide, be sure to tell him what kind of hunt you are after and ask him if he can provide it. A good guide will tell you his limitations and explain to you what he can provide.

A few years ago I planned a hunt out west for mule deer. I wrote to more than 40 guide services explaining very specific goals. I wanted three things; a) the opportunity to shoot a 30-inch buck; b) to learn western hunting; and c) to be able to guide myself with a "drop camp" in years following. In other words, I wanted to come and learn from a professional guide and then in following years be dropped off to hunt on my own. I received a lot of responses, but the guide I choose was the one who told me that a "30 inch" buck was highly unlikely anywhere out west. He explained why and told me about his best trophy areas and recent history, but that all he could offer was a good hunt and his best effort. That bit of honesty sold me on this particular guide!

2. Ask About Options and Suggestions

Guides are in the "customer service" business. They, even more than you, want to make sure that you have a good hunt. They know that a successful hunt will mean more business from you and your friends in later years. There is also the pride factor. No guide wants to come home empty handed. Whenever a man places upon himself the label of "guide", he has claimed a great deal for himself. Every day is an exam day for that man.

For this reason, it is a good idea to ask them what they would suggest concerning a great hunt. They might choose an option you haven't thought about and set a goal that you would prefer.

3. Ask for References

A good guide will have a good track record. Ask about his latest hunt and what happened. Get the guide to talk about what happened in some detail and then ask for that specific client's name and phone number as a reference. Ask for other references. Some unethical guides will give you a relative's phone number as a reference. Getting the guide to talk about his latest hunt and then using that as a reference will help you avoid the few shyster guides that you must look out for. When you call the references, ask the former client the following questions.

1. *Did the hunt meet your expectations?*
2. *Was the guide knowledgeable?*
3. *Did you learn anything about hog hunting?*
4. *How much game did you see?*
5. *What kind of hunting did you do? (Stand, Still, Bow, Gun, etc.)*
6. *Was the guide polite? What was his language like? Was he "professional"? Would he be the kind of guide that you could bring your child along?*
7. *Were there any hidden costs?*
8. *What were the facilities like? What was the land like?*
9. *Was the guide "ethical"?*
10. *Would you go there again or look for a different guide? Why?*

4. Understand the Guarantees and Conditions

Most hog hunts are either "no kill, no pay hunts" or at least "no opportunity, no pay hunts." Deer hunts on private lands are difficult to guarantee. If I were a guide, I would never guarantee a deer. Quail, ducks, and hogs are different. These hunts should have some type of guarantee system. If not, there is some reason to question the amount of hogs present or the knowledge of the guide.

Some preserves and guides require payment if a hog is wounded but not recovered. This helps insure that the hunter they guide will be responsible. Hogs, like any game animal, deserve our best efforts. Clean kills should be the goal rather than filling the air with lead just for the opportunity.

Last year I killed a nice Georgia 8-point whitetail at 275 yards. I crawled for more than 100 yards into the middle of a cut-over to get into position. Years of experience enabled me to have the skills to accomplish this. Beginning hunters should understand their limitations and not try to do things where game will be injured and suffer. Practice on the firing range is the place to experiment, not in the field. It's a terrible feeling to wound an animal and not be able to follow-up. It's an even worse feeling for the animal.

One last thing about guided hunting. Although guided, it's still hunting. Don't expect your guide to perform miracles. There are times when even the best guides will fail. In this chapter I told you about the private lease where I saw over 200 hogs in a couple of hours time. A few weeks later I returned to that same lease to take some pictures. I did not find one hog! I almost wouldn't have believed that was possible after my first trip there. It just shows you that hunting is unpredictable and that guides can't perform miracles if the conditions are wrong.

Craig Marquette with daughter Katie on the best kind of guided wild hog hunting.

I DONT KNOW WHAT THEY SEE IN IT BUT IT WORKS EVERY TIME.

TRAPPING WILD HOGS

Everything you need to know to be successful!

Chapter Nine

- How do you build a trap? What is the secret to "multiple" capture traps?
- How do you castrate boars?
- What do you use to vaccinate hogs to improve the health of the herd?

I stood looking at the 170-pound boar just 15 feet away. He bristled and grunted menacingly. The 2 inches of visible tusks were in the forefront of my thinking as he lowered his head and stared at me. I stomped my foot at him and like a freight train he charged. All the assurances of "hogs won't attack you" were quickly forgotten as he covered those scant few yards. Just as those tusks were about to be drilled into my legs, he hit the fence! After rebounding, he ran to the opposite side of the trapper's pen with the other 40 pigs.

In those few moments, I realized a few important facts.

Hogs are very fast!

I don't know if anyone has ever put a stopwatch on a wild hog, but I guarantee you that they can run down any Olympic runner without breaking a sweat! If you're ever chased, my best advice is to shoot straight or climb quickly.

Hogs are very aggressive when cornered!

The wild hogs held in that pen were terribly afraid of me. They would gather together and climb on each other's backs to stay on the opposite side of the pen. They had two clear desires. First, to stay together. Second, to stay away. When either of those tendencies are prohibited, the hog becomes aggressive and dangerous.

Hogs are truly wild animals!

The hogs that this trapper had penned were as wild as any deer or bobcat. If penned for a long enough time, they would probably calm down in the presence of humans, but these animals would never be pets. They would always be an animal to be careful around. You would never want to enter their pen and turn your back on them. Like circus lions, they might learn to cooperate but this doesn't mean they wouldn't still eat you!

Who Traps Hogs and Why?

There are many people trapping hogs. Almost all nonprofessional trapping is done on private lands by the landowner or by hunt clubs who have leased property. These two groups have two different purposes for their trapping. The landowner is generally trying to rid himself of hogs while the hunt club is attempting to better the hunting stock by castrating boars and vaccinating hogs. There are also some individuals who do not enjoy hunting but do enjoy wild hog meat - trapping is the answer!

I've interviewed many trappers for this chapter and I have discovered a world of information. The professionals have tips that will really help you catch more hogs. If you have private land available, this chapter will teach you how to get started safely in this adventure. There is also general hog information included in this chapter that cannot be found elsewhere in the book.

Basic Elements of Trapping

What is the basic idea of hog trapping? How does it work?

Hog traps are fenced pens with a trapdoor. Bait is left in the pen and when a hog enters the pen, the door is tripped. The trapper comes to the pen, loads the hog into a truck, or castrates/vaccinates and releases the hog. Baiting and trapping on private property is legal in the state of Florida, although other states may have laws prohibiting this practice.

Are hogs game animals or "pest" exotics?

In most states, hogs have a dual status. On private lands, hogs are considered a "pest" species and may be taken without limit and in multiple ways, trapping and hunting being the primary methods. Hogs do cause a lot of damage on private property. Improved pastures, landscaping, plant nurseries, and a host of other types of cultivated property can be heavily damaged by hogs. In Sarasota County, Florida, where I live, hog traps can be found even on area golf courses. If a hog were to root on a golf green or fairway, in just a few minutes it could be destroyed. I was once invited to hunt from the roof of a home in an exclusive neighborhood, with a bow and arrow, because hogs had been destroying the backyard.

On some public lands the hogs have a "game" classification and are regulated by hunting laws. Many Wildlife Management Units have their own rules for hog hunting. Most run the hog season during general deer season and some have "height" restrictions. Generally, hogs in these areas must stand 15 inches at the shoulders to be a legal animal. There is a tendency in most areas to drop these shoulder height restrictions. Shortened seasons seem to be a better idea to help keep healthy populations on these units rather than height restrictions. The reason is that any kind of height restriction is tough to obey. It's almost impossible to tell how big a hog is while walking in the brush.

How do you make a hog trap?

A hog trap can be made in many different ways, but almost all traps look very similar. Most hog traps are approximately 6 by 10 feet and stand about 5 foot high. The sides of the trap are constructed of hog wire or some other very sturdy fencing material. In the middle of one of the sections a small door is placed that will fall and lock into place. This locking mechanism is triggered by a rope attached to the middle of the trap. When the hog pushes the rope, the door swings shut. Hog traps are normally portable, but there are some which are permanent.

Although this describes the common trap, the similarities between these traps and the "root-door" trap end. The root-door trap is far superior to other traps for a number of reasons. It is segmented, which means that more than one trap can be carried in the back of a truck. It is a trap that enables safe capture of the hogs into a trailer or truck, without having to "hog-tie" and carry the pig aboard. It is also a multiple capture trap. If you would like to receive plans, write to Florida Game and Freshwater Commission and request a copy of the plans for the "Portable Root-door Hog Trap." The trap was originally designed by Jerry Peoples and David Austin, but the paper you want to get is by Robert C. Belden and William B. Frankenberger.

What is the secret to "multiple" captures?

The main difference between the root-door trap and other traps is the door. With the "root" door a hog must push it open to gain entry. The root door is a one-way door that doesn't shut permanently once a hog

A multiple capture root-door trap!

is in the trap. This allows other hogs to enter after the first! Another secret to multiple captures is to leave the trap open for about a week so that multiple animals get used to entering it. When the door is set to the one-way position, hogs will continue to enter the trap.

How many hogs can be caught in the same trap?

My friend Bill reports that he has had as many as 17 hogs stacked in a trap, but professional trapper Jerry Peoples' personal record is absolutely amazing. Jerry told me that he has had 43 hogs in the same trap when he went to check it. That's wall-to-wall pork!

The number of hogs taken in a single trap over a period of time is really dependant upon the population of hogs present. Normally, there is one hog for about every 13-16 acres in good habitat in Florida, but this percentage differs greatly. There are some areas in Florida with very few hogs, although hogs are found in every county of the state. Jerry told me that he catches about 70-80 hogs each time he checks his traps. He runs about 12 traps. If you can maintain a 2 hog per trap average over an extended period, you're doing good!

Do traps need a top ceiling section?

Many people use a top section but it is really unneeded. One reason is that top sections trap deer that would normally jump out. If a top is used and a deer is trapped, the deer will probably kill itself running into the sides in panic as you approach to let it loose. Also, professional trappers report that they lose only about 1 hog out of 250 hogs by loss over the top. You can carry more traps without having this top section to worry about.

How do hogs find a trap?

The secret is to leave the trap open for a week and allow hogs to begin using it. Leaving a trail of corn for a few hundred yards leading toward the trap is a good way to let hogs know where it is. Once they find it, they will quickly become accustomed to checking it for food. If you were to put a feeder over a trap for a week, you would really get them using it.

What is good hog trap bait?

Corn is the most oft used bait for hogs, although there are many, many kinds of good bait that will work. Soured corn is also sometimes used. One biologist told me that his favorite bait was stale pastries which he often received from a bakery. I also spoke to a trapper who liked to use stale potato chips. He swore that when no one else could catch hogs, he could slay them with old chips! You too might be able to work out free bait from a local bakery or food manufacturer.

Do you move traps when trapping larger sections of land?

Most hunt clubs or private land owners would probably build a trap and leave it in the same place, but to really get serious about removing hogs, traps need to be moved. The method most often used by experts is to have multiple lines drawn on the property. For example, a line of traps on the south boundary would be placed first and baited in the "open" position for one week. Then these traps would be "set" to be sprung and a new set of traps would be set on the north boundary and baited for two weeks while hogs are being captured on the south boundary. Then the north boundary traps are set and used while the south boundary traps are moved to the east boundary and baited "un-set" for two weeks. This leapfrog method of trapping should be used across the property. Thus, a systematic system is used to cover the whole area.

Can hogs be eradicated?

Only on a closed area. For example, if you own an island off the coast that has hogs, they can be eradicated. Or, if you own a piece of land bordered by a development or if you own land in an area with very poor habitat surrounding your land, it might be possible. Generally these are the only situations that would allow for hog eradication.

On most land "hog control" is the answer. One Florida Cracker told me, "we will have hogs and coyotes for as long as there is a Florida." Hog control is the main goal, not hog eradication.

Biologists tell me that at least 70% of the hogs must be removed to make a real impact on hog damage being done. Hog control, after reaching 70%, must be continued to make sure that the problem does not return. This can only be accomplished by using systematic trapping and hunting. Hunting is needed because some hogs learn about traps and will never be caught in them. To really control hogs, landowners need to be pro-active and have both methods used on their property.

Is trapping dangerous? How do you get hogs out of the trap and into the truck?

Hogs can be very dangerous. A trapped hog is a cornered wild animal. He wants to get loose and he knows that you prevent him from doing so. A system can be developed to make direct contact with wild hogs rare. The secret is making a shoot (tunnel-like area going from the trap to the truck or trailer) via a door that attaches to your trap. This door too should be a one-way door to prevent hogs from going both ways. When you empty the trap, you will drive up to the trap, attach the shoot, and spook the hog into the truck or trailer. When you get to the home pen, you reverse the process and spook the hogs back down the shoot. The door can be attached in two different directions to prevent unexpected releases. An electric cattle prod can be used to spook an unspookable hog! A rope can also be used to pull the hog into the truck, but this gets to be a bit of a tough tug-of-war!

How can a hog hurt you?

Hogs have three major ways that they can cause you harm (other than the diseases that you can catch from them). They can gore and slash with tusks. They can bite like the worst pitbull you've ever met. And they can kick and push. The way that most people get hurt is by being bitten by a hog. I heard the story of a big boar that had been caught, hog-tied and placed in the back of a truck. The trapper reached in the back of the truck to get something and put his hand too close to the hog's mouth. The hog almost bit the man's hand off. Major damage can be done by hogs and great care needs to be taken when in their presence. Another story I heard concerned a man whose main leg tendon was slashed by a boar. Always be careful when in their presence!

What is a "Bar" hog? Why do boars need to be castrated?

A "bar" hog is a castrated hog. Technically, it means a hog castrated before reaching sexual maturity. A stag is a hog castrated after reaching sexual maturity. But hunters use the term "bar" to refer to both.

Boars are castrated because it causes them to grow larger and helps to sweeten the meat. "Common knowledge" among hog hunters is that boars are not worth the trouble it takes to gut and prepare them. As with many other things we've heard, we think this wisdom could be somewhat exagerated. The age of the hog is the predominant factor in determining quality of taste. There are bad boars, but not all boars are bad!

How do you castrate a boar?

After trapping the hog, get a rope around his neck and pull him to the side of the trap. It would probably be safest to get two ropes around the hog, one around the neck and one around one of the back legs. Get the hog disabled near the side of the trap by keeping the legs tied up in the air and stretched in different directions. Reach inside the trap and grab the testicles of the hog and slice the scrotum so that the testicles can be pulled out and cut off. A bit of disinfectant is used to prevent infection. (A clip can be placed around the testicles which causes the same thing to happen over time). Use a knife to cut off half the hogs ear to mark him as a "bar." That way, when released, hunters on your property will know which boars have been castrated and which have not.

How does castration affect the hog's behavior?

Castrating the boar causes him to lose his sex drive. He will probably begin to travel with other "bars" and go into a nocturnal mode (wouldn't you go into a nocturnal mode if someone did that to your testicles?). See chapter 4, Hog Habits, for more details on barrow hog behavior.

Can you pen and "fatten-up" hogs?

This is more difficult to do than you might imagine. A hog's natural diet and the diet you will feed him are very different. If you feed him corn or grain he will get the "scours," a diarrhea-like condition. It is caused by the digestive system not having the necessary bacteria to digest the food from the new diet. Thus, the hog must be introduced to new feed gradually. Hog feed might solve the problem. If you don't want to go with store-bought feed, soaking corn in water for a time will help the hogs begin to be able to digest it. Hogs will eat any "slop" fed to them, but again, diarrhea is a real potential problem.

Another thing to think about before doing this is the fact that hogs are the leanest possible pork that can be found. If you "fatten" them, they will lose this natural "lean." Fattening them is generally unnecessary. The only time I would recommend this procedure is if you have caught a boar and want to improve his taste a little. Then, I would castrate him and hold him 5-6 weeks before slaughter. Otherwise, feeding hogs is unneeded. They are the best pork available!

How do you "hog-tie" a hog?

Have you ever grabbed a running chainsaw at the wrong end? If you attempt this maneuver and fail, you might think you did! It is difficult to imagine that you can successfully perform this without watching it first. I recommend that you learn from someone who knows what they are doing. The basic procedure is to grab the rear leg (maybe while a friend holds the head with a rope) and pick the leg off the ground. When you have the leg, you have control of the hog. You must lift the hog off the ground and as he falls place your leg across his neck, at the same time keeping the leg under control. Once in this position, you can grab the legs and tie each leg together.

Are hogs safe once hog-tied or penned?

Hogs are always dangerous. They can be very aggressive. The State of Florida Game Commission once even had two cases reported in a neighborhood where a hog attacked children to take food away from them. These hogs had been fed by neighbors and had lost their fear of people. The hog was successful on his first attempt at robbing a child and decided to try it again.

How do you vaccinate hogs? What should be used?

Hunters who want to make the hogs on their property healthier and heavier should be vaccinating their hogs. The trappers I know like to use "Ivermectine." They measure 1 ml per 20 pounds of hog and shoot it into the neck. There is about an 80-90% success rate of ridding the hog of parasites. This causes average weights to really increase on your hunting lease.

Is there a right way to approach a pen? What happens when a trap is approached?

Remember that traps are normally set for two weeks in the "open" position to get many hogs coming to the trap. When the trap is set in

Guide Matt Scarbrough inoculates a piglet!

this "open" position, it should be approached from the rear! The reason for this is simple, it allows a deer or bear or even a hog to exit the trap and not to become cornered. If a deer is cornered, the deer could easily kill itself in a panic. One trapper told me that this was the #1 mistake that amateur trappers make. If a bear or hog is in an open door trap -- you might be killed. Approach these "open" traps from the rear.

When you approach a trap and there are hogs present, you can expect a panic on your hands. The hogs will ram themselves into the sides of the trap trying to escape. It is obvious by this that they are used to running through whatever they decide to run through. This can really cut up the face of the hog, but generally does no permanent damage. After bouncing off the sides of the trap, they generally stay to the far end away from you, except for the occasional charge as you get the shoot ready to put them into the truck. (See question on putting hogs into trucks).

How often do hog traps need to be checked?

At least 3 times a week, depending on the time of year. In extremely hot periods, it might be good to check the traps every day or every other day, but generally a few times a week is sufficient.

What are the laws concerning the selling of hogs?

Wild hogs can be sold, but the rules governing this are fairly strict. This is because of the diseases that can be transmitted to domestic hogs or to the "buyers" themselves. Generally, wild hogs must be "dead" when they leave your facility. Check the laws in your state or region to find out specifically what the law requires.

Where can they be sold?

Hogs can be sold where other hogs are sold - at auctions across the state. They can also be sold from your backyard or along the side of the road! They just can't be sold "out-of-state."

Who would want to buy a wild hog?

Many people, once they try "wild hog", develop a real taste for it. Many people like buying a small hog for barbeques. Normally, the seller must skin and butcher the hog, but some people will want to buy the hog whole.

Many hunt preserves buy live wild hogs to place on their property. For a landowner attempting to get rid of hogs from his property, he might contact a hunt preserve to see if they would be interested in some hogs.

Can they be shipped "out-of-state"?

It is very difficult to ship hogs out-of-state. Most states require vaccination and health documents to do this. There is sometimes a quarantine period where the health of the animal must be proved. Since there are diseases that wild hogs can carry into domestic hog populations, states are very careful about not infecting their livestock with diseases that may not be presently a problem.

Can a person make a living trapping hogs?

Professional trapper Jerry Peoples says that there is a living to be made, but the life is tough and the work is difficult. If someone loves being in the "outdoors" and has a strong work ethic and a lot of integrity, this would be a great job. Integrity is needed because large landowners need help with hogs, but are particular about protecting their deer, turkey, and livestock. If a trapper takes advantage of his access and hunts anything but hogs, he quickly loses his reputation through "word-of-mouth" advertising and no other landowners will trust him or work with him.

Trapping is o.k., but we prefer to get our hogs the old fashioned way, with a well-placed 30-06!

I USE POODLES FOR THE BIG FAT RICH ONES AND DALMATIONS FOR THE TOUGH FIREMEN AND STEEL WORKERS

Dogs and Hogs

Chapter Ten

- What are the best dogs for hog hunting?
- What is the difference between "cold" nose dogs and "hot" nose dogs?
- Which are better dogs, hounds or catch dogs?
- How do you train blood-trail dogs?

Jim left his dogs at home because his friend Buck was bringing the "pits" (pitbulls). The day began slowly, but suddenly the sound of a dog pack in hot pursuit broke the morning silence and signaled a change of luck. Dogs howling, hogs squealing, brush busting as the hunters ran after the hogs - this was what it's all about!

Jim and Buck approached the sound of dogs fighting and growling with great enthusiasm. The lead dog had the hog by the ear and wasn't letting go. The others were attached like "ticks" at various places on the hog. Jim and Buck hog-tied the porker and pulled the dogs off. One man held the dogs on leash while the other put the hog on a carrier to get out of the woods. The morning's hunt was a great success!

THE THRILL OF THE HUNT

Dog hunting for hogs is a world unto itself. The process is rather simple: find the scent trail of a hog; start the dogs in the correct direction; catch or "bay" the hog; and then, harvest or castrate and release the hog. Watching and following the action of the dogs is as much an attraction as the actual dealings with the hog. In this regard, it is much like bird hunting. There's not many things more beautiful than watching a perfect point on a covey and there's not many things more exciting than following the chase of the hog. It is like "coon" hunting but the hog has a very real chance of killing a dog!

As in all sports, there are variables that come into play. For instance, warm or cold scent trails, night or day hunting, hounds or catch dogs, and so on. We will cover these in more detail, but it suffices to say that this is one exciting form of hunting. Be sure you take the opportunity to hunt with a professional guide if you don't have access to dog hunting. This type of hunting is a thrill that you don't want to miss!

Hey Dixie, I've got the back, YOU grab the front!

How Did Dogs Come to Hunt with Men?

Dogs just plain love to hunt! As far back as recorded history, man has used dogs and their natural God-given abilities to hunt and capture game. To understand a little of what lurks within a hunting dog, we need to go no further than the nature television programs. We've all seen the familiar scene of a wolf pack circling a weakened prey, then forging in for the meal. Members of the canine family hunt in "packs." They cooperate with each other to capture game. There is only one member of the cat family that hunts in this way, the lions. Cats are normally "solitary" predators whereas canines are "team" hunters. Man captured dogs, tamed them, and used their "team" instincts to help with the hunt. This natural instinct to hunt with others has been strengthened by selective breeding. Hunting dog breeders notice a "desirable" trait and breed to increase the likelihood of that trait showing up in their litters. This is how dog breeders develop a breed to do a specific job.

How Do Dogs "Scent" Animals and Trail Them?

Whenever an animal walks on the ground, scent particles are left on the ground. If the animal stops in a certain area, a "scent cone" spreads out from where it is located. Dogs have the great ability to not only tell that something walked a certain trail, but differentiate which animal walked it. The scent of an animal or person is as distinctive to a dog as fingerprints are to us. If you've watched television shows, you might think that jumping into a creek or lake is a good way to "fool" a dog. Don't waste your time! A well-trained dog will be able to smell the scent particles that have flowed from the middle of the creek to the banks. In other words, a good dog can trail you even up or down a creek or river. There are even dogs, used by police, that are used to find drowned bodies. The dogs are trained to sniff a lake and alert their masters to the presence of a drowned victim under the surface of the water. This kind of dog is used when a small child or very elderly person is lost and it is feared that they have fallen into some local water source. Dogs have an amazing ability to see with their noses!

The Hounds

Hounds are dogs that have been selectively bred for a specific purpose. Hounds are bred to bark loudly while chasing (so that the hunters can follow) and to have a great sense of smell (all dogs have great noses, but hounds have this ability to an even greater degree). Hounds are also generally bred to "bay" game. Baying means to "corner" game rather than catch it.

Advantages to Hog Hunting with Hounds

- ***Hounds have the special ability of being able to follow cold trails.***

Cold trails are those that are older than about two hours. They are thus considered to have cold noses. Hounds also have the tenacity to stay on a trail for many hours. Sometimes dogs are lost for a time because they won't give up the chase. You might realize that it's time to go home for dinner before the wife gets mad, but I guarantee you that your dog won't care. Why should he? At worst, you will be in the dog house with him!

I was hunting in Georgia many years ago when a totally "orange" dressed man came running through the woods past me. About an hour later I looked up to see a uniformed guard being led through the woods by a bloodhound puppy on leash. I stopped the guard and asked what was going on and was told that they were training a new dog for the correctional facility nearby. When the dog matured, he told me, he would be able to cold-trail a convict on a trail that was as much as 24 hours or more old.

- ***Hounds can be followed and understood by their barks.***

Hounds use different kinds of barks and howls to signal different situations in the field. When the dog is searching, he has a certain bark, but as he picks up the trail and begins the chase there is a distinctive change in the howl of the dog. As the race nears completion, many owners can tell by the enthusiasm of the barks and howls what is going on. Many dog hunters "commentate" the chase as they follow the hunt. Some of these hunters are pretty good "play-by-play" specialists, although some tend to exaggerate the skills of their favorite dog.

- ***Hounds can be used in low-density hog areas.***

Since hounds can "scent" very old trails, they can be used in areas that have few hogs. Driving the truck down old dirt roads until a fresh track is found, then releasing the hounds, is a good way to find hogs. Catch dogs are not nearly as good at scenting old trails and can become frustrated in low-density areas.

- ***Hounds do not damage hogs because they "bay" rather than catch.***

Hounds are better dogs for guides or hunt clubs because they do not actually catch the hogs. The hogs remain unscarred and are more "mountable" as trophies. If a hunt club or private lease wanted to increase the health of their herd very quickly, hound hunting would do this without harming the marketability of the hogs.

Catch Dogs

Catch dogs generally run down hogs silently and catch them and hold them for the hunter to arrive. Catching hogs is a little dangerous. Hogs are as good at slashing and biting as catch dogs are at locking on and not letting go! The most common type of catch dog used is the infamous pitbull! Catch dogs must be put onto trails that are somewhat fresh or "warm." Most catch dogs need a trail that is not older than 2 hours old to be successful at finding the hog.

Advantages to Hog Hunting with Catch Dogs

- ***Catch dogs are fearless and will tackle any hog in the woods.***

Big boars can kill a dog quickly and a good catch dog is the "equalizer" in these kinds of situations. A pack of dogs usually has a "lead" dog which will attempt to grab the hog first. A good catch dog is a real advantage when the pack approaches because he is designed to get in there and quickly win the fight.

- ***Catch dogs "catch" hogs more quickly than hounds.***

Since most breeds of catch dogs chase with little or no barking, the hog doesn't know that the dog is coming until it's too late. If your goal is to enjoy the chase, then you should buy a hound. If your goal is catching the greatest number of hogs per hunt, then catch dogs are the answer.

- ***Catch dogs actually "catch" the hog.***

How do you like the idea of tackling an unhindered wild hog face-to-face which has been riled up and maddened by a pack of dogs barking and chasing it? Catch dogs are great because they incapacitate the hog and get him under control when you approach. If you use hounds, the hog is "cornered" but is able to charge or run. I talked to one old-timer who was on a horse when a bayed hog attacked and slashed the stomach region out of his horse. The horse died! Having the hog under control is a real advantage!

General Questions on Dog Hunting

What are the best dogs to get for hog hunting?

There are as many opinions on "best" kinds of dogs as there are hunters. If you are new to hog hunting with dogs, we highly recommend "Plott-hounds" or "Airedales" or crosses between the two. The Catahoula Leopard dogs are also fearless. These dogs are hot for hogs! Bird-dog crosses are also good because they are generally much faster than hounds and still have great noses. We freely admit that any good hunting stock hound can become a great hog dog! There is no standard dog and you can develop your own with smart cross-breeding.

How are hog dogs trained?

The dog should be at least 8 months old and weigh more than 35 pounds before they are allowed to chase hogs. If a young dog is hurt on his first outing, he may become "hog-shy" and avoid contact. The secret to all dog training is setting the dog up for success.

Trophy boar taken with a Plott hound!

I have a friend who trains dogs for the police. I once asked him how he trains his dogs to fight and capture vicious criminals who shoot at, kick, and fight the dogs. His answer amazed me! He said that every day, he found someone to "fake" fight his dogs. He would find someone to put on the "arm-pad" or "full-body suit." Before every fight, he would instruct his accomplice to fight, but to "lose" in the end. His police dogs were undefeated! They thought they were the baddest dogs walking the earth! Every day they got into a fight and every day they won the fight! The dogs are conditioned to believe that they can't lose a fight. Good dog trainers set their dogs up for success rather than failure. This basic principle needs to be kept in mind when training hog dogs.

This means that you should introduce your dog to an experienced pack where he can go along and see what he needs to do by watching other dogs succeed. If you don't have access to an experienced pack, it would be smart to trap a small hog and let your dog catch it a few times. As he gains successful experiences, he will become more bold and soon be all the dog that you need for any situation!

How long can you hunt a dog on a hot day?

Hunting dogs are athletes. If they have been exercised properly, they will hunt for hours and hours and not get tired. Heat exhaustion is always a concern. Be sure that you rest your dogs on really hot days and make sure that a water source is available for drinking.

What is the best time to hunt hogs, day or night?

It's a personal matter, but hands down, I prefer the day! There are hearty souls who brave the darkness for several reasons. One would be that hogs are active at night and fresh trails are easy to find. Many pressured areas produce mostly nocturnal hogs. Another reason would be the excitement of not being able to see which end of the hog you are about to grab (this thrill escapes me). A friend of mine was once night-hunting with a buddy and there was only one flashlight between them. As the men got hold of the first hog, the dogs took off after another. My friend was left holding the bag (a 125-pound boar) without the benefit of a flashlight. He had only one rear leg (which is enough to control a hog) but could not see to tie the hog. After a long wait, he decided to see if he could hog-tie a hog blindfolded! Unfortunately, it was he rather than the hog who was blind. He did succeed but expressed to me hesitation in trying this maneuver again!

What equipment is needed for dog hunting?

A dog box in your car or truck to put your muddy or bloodied dogs in to get them home. A good leash is needed to hold the dogs after the hog has been captured. It also helps to get the pack back to the truck after you've decided the hunt is over. If not, you might be hunting your dogs, rather than hogs, to get them home in time for dinner or maybe even breakfast.

Snake boots or chaps are a good idea to own. They slow you down and make you a bit more sweaty but it gives a peace of mind that, to my way of thinking, is worth the negatives. Rope is needed to hog-tie the captured hogs and a method of getting the hog out of the woods is also needed (see chapter 12 for some suggestions). A surgical stitch kit is also important to have along!

I've heard of "chest protectors" for dogs. These are leather aprons put around the dog which help protect the dog from being gored or slashed. This is a good idea for your lead dog. I don't know of any commercially made aprons, but a good leather worker can make a custom fitted one just for your dog.

What about radio collars?

There are two types of radio collars. One is a "shock" collar that is used for dog training. These can be purchased in outdoor mail-order magazines and start at about $200. There isn't a lot of use for training collars for hog dogs, but they can be used to snake proof your dogs. These kinds of collars are generally used for bird-dog training.

The second type of radio collar is used to find a distant dog. They are "directional" collars, also called "homing" collars, which tell the master where the hunt is taking place. The collars are good for certain distances, depending on the money you are willing to spend. Some are good for finding your dogs at more than 5 miles! If you've ever known the frustration of a lost dog and the hours that you put into finding them, you understand the value of this collar.

Blood-Trail Dogs

Trail dogs are allowed on most public lands, even if "dog hunting" is not allowed. The trail dog must be kept in the truck until after the shot and then must only be used on leash.

Trail dogs can follow the scent of a wounded hog, even if there is no visible blood trail. Good dogs follow wounded animals and differentiate them from other hogs because gasses from the body cavity escape and a scent trail is laid that man is incapable of sensing!

If you have a good trail dog - you can also make some money! Offer your phone number at differing wildlife management units in your area, and charge $35-50 an attempt! People will call you if they've lost a wounded hog. If your dog is good, you will quickly get plenty of business.

How to Train Trail Dogs!

Any good hunting dog can become a hog trail dog, but hounds are especially good because of their breeding. I personally like training my "duck lab" to trail hogs and I think he enjoys this dual role. He gets into the field more often and loves the challenge!

Basic Trail Dog Training Principles

Here are the basic steps to training a trail dog.

1) As a puppy, get the dog to play with a tennis ball or some other soft fetch toy. Teach him to fetch and enjoy this game. Always end the game when the dog is still excited and eager. Keep and store the

special "fetch" toy away from him at all other non-training times. This means that he is always excited to "see" it and associates it with extreme fun!

2) When the puppy loves to fetch, make him sit and watch you as you hide the toy. Let him now fetch by going to get the toy that he has just seen you hide. Encourage him to search in this way by saying to him, "find him" or "where is he" or "fetch it up." When he does find it, get excited and praise him. Throw the ball for him to fetch as a reward for finding it. Never overdo this training, keep him eager!

3) Make the game more difficult by hiding the toy in one place while pretending to hide it in other places. Walk around the whole room acting like you are putting the tennis ball in various holes, crevices, and under various pillows. Release him with a command and remember to reward him with praise and a game of fetch each time he succeeds.

4) Make the game even more difficult by commanding the dog to stay while you go into another room to hide the toy. The puppy is now beginning to understand that his job is to find things when you tell him. Reward him with praise, play, and excitement every time he succeeds.

5) At some time in the process of this training - begin keeping the ball in a plastic freezer bag with a piece of hog hide in it. Make sure that the ball smells like a hog. Your wife might prefer that this training take place outside the house, rather than inside. He will begin to associate hog smell with searching and finding and excitement and fun!

6) Take the dog hunting with you. When someone kills a hog and has already found it, bring the dog into the woods and command him to search for the hog. Start him where the hog was shot and let him follow the hog's trail till he gets to the hog. Praise him highly when he finds the hog. Pull out his ball and reward him by playing some fetch. Let someone drag the hog toward the truck and let your dog follow him to the truck! Set your dog up for success.

Don't put him on a real lost trail until he truly understands what his job is to be. This might discourage him. This is the basic process of training a trailing dog. A good trailing dog will be worth his weight in gold to special weapons hunters. You might even love the "search" as much as hunting hogs themselves!

Dave blood-trail training his yellow lab Dixie!

YOU MUST TAKE PROPER PRECAUTIONS TO KEEP FROM CATCHING HUMAN DISEASES.
-Always practice safe field dressing
-Always practice safe cooking
-Always wear rubber gloves

WILD HOG DISEASES

Chapter Eleven

- With what diseases do hunters need to be concerned? Is hog brucellosis truly more dangerous than bovine brucellosis?
- What diseases and health issues are there for our dogs and livestock?

The more than 60 year old trapper began his career with hogs at the tender age of 8. When your father is a trapper, it almost comes naturally. Never had the old trapper taken any precautions when dealing with hogs and he had seen and handled thousands upon thousands of them. One afternoon he was hired to guide some hunters. The hunt was successful and 8 hogs were killed. The old trapper gutted and cleaned them like the professional that he was. The average man couldn't have cleaned a single hog before he had all cut and gutted. Because they were deep on a private lease, they were not near a water source. The old trapper used grass and leaves to clean his bloody hands. As he rubbed them, he remembered putting up some barbed-wire fence that morning. Now his hands were really scratched and beaten. Thirty days later, this trapper had a new problem, learning how to manage a debilitating, lifetime, incurable disease called brucellosis!

BRUCELLOSIS

ALL HUNTERS BEWARE!

Have you ever dreamed of having malaria? Probably not! You've probably never imagined that you could get malaria. Our mosquitos don't carry malaria, right? I'm not a malaria expert, but I would guess that Americans have little chance of catching malaria, but let me be clear, THERE IS A HIGH PROBABILITY OF HUNTERS CATCHING BRUCELLOSIS.

The #1 thing I learned while researching this book is that I've been foolish and ignorant concerning this disease. My hunting practices will never be the same because of it.

Different types of brucellosis are found in hogs, goats, and cattle. Bovine brucellosis (found in cattle) is not very severe and nothing much to be worried about in humans. It can be controlled very adequately with antibiotics. I don't know anything about goat brucellosis, but HOG BRUCELLOSIS CAN KILL YOU! It is incurable and only the symptoms can be treated.

How Brucellosis Affects the Hog!

Hogs catch brucellosis by eating infected material (like the afterbirth of piglets or the remains of other hogs, remember that hogs eat carrion {dead animals} and anything else they can find), breathing infected air after another hog coughs or sneezes, by being punctured by the tusks of an infected hog, or by sex! Like most dangerous diseases, hogs catch it primarily through sex. How about a "safe sex" program for hogs????

Brucellosis may cause sows to abort, or cause infertility in males. In advanced cases, hogs may become lame. The hogs sometimes develop abscesses (some as large as footballs). Common areas to find these are in the testicles or female tract regions (be careful when castrating or spaying).

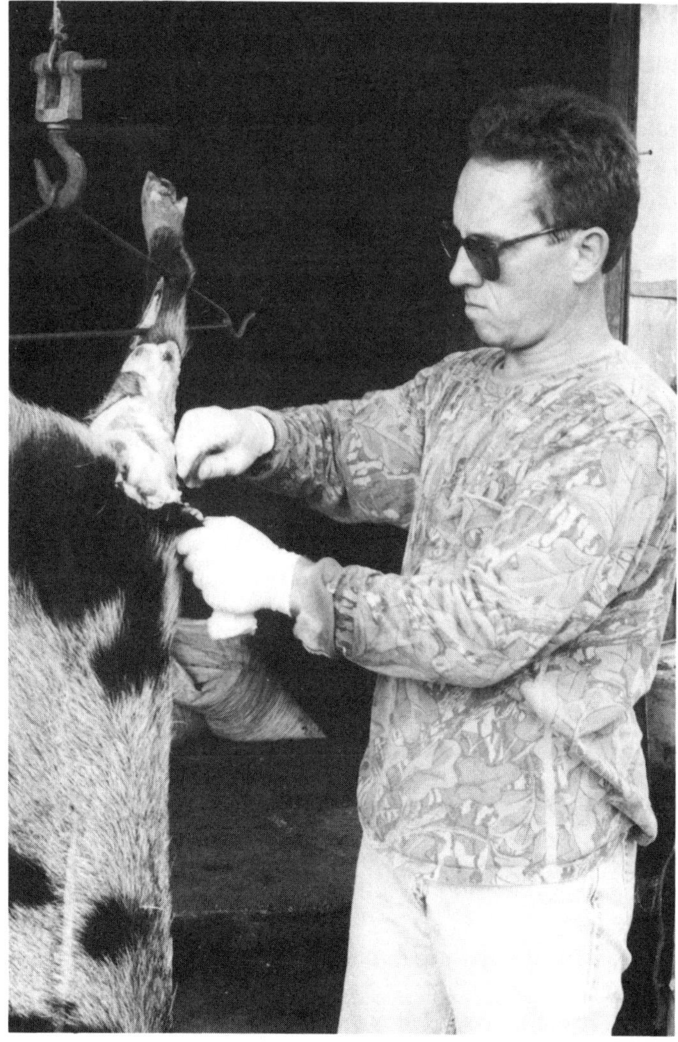

Don't chance contracting brucellosis, wear gloves!

The disease is very widespread among hogs. In a study done on Fish Eating Creek, Florida, more than 50% of the adult hogs were infected with brucellosis. Other studies have shown an almost 90% infection rate. In a 1993 study, hogs were collected from 19 sites across the state of Florida. Brucellosis was confirmed or strongly suspected at 10 of those sites. Nine of those sites were clear of brucellosis. Of the 10 sites where brucellosis was found, about 25% of the hogs had the disease. In other words, you will come into contact with brucellosis if you hunt hogs over your lifetime.

How Brucellosis Affects You!

The story at the beginning of this chapter is a true story. I interviewed an old Florida Cracker who had brucellosis. He had trapped hogs for 32 years without taking any preventative measures. He told me that he always "reasoned" that if he were susceptible, he would have already caught the disease after so many years of trapping, hunting, and cleaning hogs. This old-timer, in his heyday, captured more than 3,000 hogs per year! At the age of 48 he came down with what he thought was a bad case of the flu. After the flu did not disappear, doctors began to suspect that he might have developed a rare case of leukemia. The doctors were wrong. He had finally contracted brucellosis. After reading a description of the symptoms, while he was planning on dying because of the rapid decline in his health, he realized that he needed to be tested for brucellosis.

He describes the symptoms of brucellosis as flu-like; severe headaches, fever, and chills were the initial problems. As time passed, he became listless and began to lose weight. After discovering the actual disease, doctors treated him with antibiotics. Today he is unable to hold down a steady job because the severe headaches remain and affect him weekly.

In another recent case, a man died after contracting what doctors thought was a rare blood disease. The autopsy revealed that the disease was actually brucellosis. This man was not a hunter so doctors made no tests to check for it before he died. The man's wife then remembered about a year earlier, a friend brought a wild hog to the house and asked her husband to help clean it. The hunter then gave a part of the hog to the man. This practice of cleaning hogs without proper protection cost the man his life! Although rarely fatal, this disease can greatly affect you.

How to Avoid Brucellosis!

Body fluids are the thing to avoid. Like AIDS, brucellosis is caught by a transfer of body fluids, or, unlike AIDS, by breathing infected matter. You don't have to have scratched or cut hands to catch the disease.

Here are the major rules to avoid catching brucellosis.

1) Do not clean pigs if you have open sores or wounds on your hands or body. Pay a friend to do it!
2) Always wear disposable rubber gloves when dressing wild pigs. Avoid all contact with body fluids and realize that the reproductive organs are hot spots to be careful around. Keep gloves in your backpack or truck!
3) As soon as possible, wash hands with soap and hot water after cleaning pigs.
4) Burn or bury gloves and remains from pigs. This prevents dogs or other animals from eating infected matter.
5) Cook meat thoroughly. Know that the meat is still dangerous until it is frozen or cooked!

Pseudorabies

What your dog needs to worry about!

Pseudorabies, also commonly known as Aujeszkys disease, is not hog rabies. **It does not cause the hog to go crazy and humans cannot catch it.** It is a very serious hog disease that is found throughout feral hog populations and, like brucellosis, is transmitted primarily through sex. In domestic swine, infections result in a high piglet mortality, central nervous system problems, as well as fever, anorexia and abortions in females. Wild swine do not exhibit these symptoms but do carry and transmit the disease to domestic swine.

The issue for hunters is that this disease can be caught by dogs, cats, cattle, sheep, and goats. In these animals, sickness usually results in central nervous disfunctions (frenzy, paralysis, and drooling). Pseudorabies is fatal for these animals and can be caught by breathing or eating infected hog material or by being wounded by a hog. There is no inoculation for the disease.

The Journal of Wildlife Diseases published a report saying that 13 sites were studied. Of those 13 sites, infected wild hogs were found in 11 of them. In the adult population, a full 70% of the hogs carried this disease. In juveniles, only 20% had contracted the disease.

Other Health Concerns

There are a number of parasites that can infect wild hogs. No common feral hog parasites are harmful to humans. The precautions mentioned in this chapter are not only to be taken with hogs, but with all wild game. Many other animals carry diseases that can be caught by man. Most common North American game species are free of diseases that are easily transmittable to humans, but I like to play it safe and always take the proper precautions. Just because the hunting culture is generally unconcerned does not mean that there is not a real threat to your health and the health of your family, especially with hogs.

WILD·HOG·HUNTERS

BE·AWARE!

FLORIDA·WILD·HOGS·MAY·INFECT·YOU·WITH

SWINE · BRUCELLOSIS

Hunting wild hogs is a long-standing tradition with Florida hunters. These popular game animals are found in almost every county of the state, and during the 1980-81 hunting season, more than 20,000 hunters killed more than 100,000 of them.

Until recent scientific studies were made of Florida's wild hog population, it was not known that perhaps half of them could have brucellosis, and that hunters might become infected with this disease when these game animals are dressed.

If you have dressed wild hogs, and have symptoms of illness that may be similar to kidney problems or that may be similar to flu symptoms (headaches, fever, muscle soreness, nausea or breathing difficulties), see your physician. A simple blood test can diagnose swine brucellosis in humans.

PRECAUTIONS WHICH MAY REDUCE RISK:

1. Always wear disposable plastic or rubber gloves when dressing and cleaning wild hogs. Keep several pair in your field hunting supply kit. Avoid direct contact with blood whenever possible.
2. As soon as possible, wash with soap and hot water after dressing wild hogs.
3. Gloves and remains from dressing wild hogs should be buried or burned.
4. Meat from wild hogs should always be thoroughly cooked before consumption.

FLORIDA GAME AND FRESH WATER FISH COMMISSION

This public document was promulgated at an annual cost of $70, or $0.35 each to provide information to Florida hunters about brucellosis.

Your friends might not believe what we've said about wild hog diseases, but the State of Florida does!

LET'S TAKE
THIS ONE HOME
AND
FATTEN HIM UP.

From Last Breath to Ice Box

How to Get Your Hog from the Field to the Freezer!

Chapter Twelve

- How do you field-dress and skin a hog?
- How do you get your hog out of the woods and into your truck?
- How long will wild hog meat "keep" in the freezer?

Whenever I take someone new hunting with me, I always give them the same parting advice. The advice is simple, clear cut, and cannot be misunderstood. I always tell them, "Here's the deal! If you shoot your hog properly, in the chest area, forward of the diaphragm, I will clean your hog for you and show you how it's done. If, on the other hand, you gut-shoot your hog and make a mess of his vitals, I will gladly explain to you from a distance how to field-dress him." It doesn't take Daniel Boone to figure out that a properly hit hog is easy to clean and a poorly hit one is a stinking mess to deal with. Choose your shots carefully!

Hog Down, Now What?

Wild hog is delicious when the proper precautions are taken in the field as well as in the kitchen. More meat is ruined by mishandling than any other reason. In the field you must have a sharp knife (preferably a sharpener along too) and rubber gloves for field dressing the hog. Because of the brucellosis threat, gloves are needed from field dressing until in the freezer (see chapter 11 on Hog Diseases).

Because most wild hogs are killed in the deep south (75% of all hogs in the United States are in Texas and Florida), high temperatures are common. The animal should be dressed as quickly as possible after it is found. When temperatures are very low, in the 40's or below, the meat will probably remain good for 10 hours or more, but when temperatures are high, spoiled meat can occur in a shorter time.

Field Dressing

- First, put on your rubber gloves!
- Roll the hog to it's back with the rump lower than the shoulders. This helps with drainage of the guts.
- Find the anus and you are not going to believe this, but stick your finger in slightly and pinch the 'tube' of the anus (remember you do have rubber gloves on). Get a grip on the anus and cut around the tube. The initial incision through the outer skin will be tough, but once through, the knife should slice around the tube nicely.
- Cut around the tube as deeply as possible, continuing to drive the knife deeper and deeper without cutting the tube of the anus. After cutting, some people tie the anus shut with a piece of string so that feces will not fall out into the body cavity when pulled through, but this is probably unneeded, because any lost feces will be quickly

removed in a moment.

- Make a cut along the center of the belly from the breast bone to the pelvic bone. In males, you will have to cut around the testicles.
- Reach into the pelvic region and pull the anus and bladder through to the body cavity and out. It might be necessary to cut around the anal tube from the inside. Pull gently but firmly and if your outside cuts were deep enough, it should pull through.
- Roll the hog onto his side and roll the stomach and intestines out onto the ground.
- Cut the diaphragm which separates the chest area from the stomach cavity, then reach into the hog, up to your elbows, and cut the windpipe lose.
- Pull the lungs and heart out. If you have shot the hog with a high powered rifle, you might have lung matter scattered throughout the chest area. Lung matter also sometimes hangs in the holes where the bones attach to the spine. Be sure to get all organ matter from the entire body cavity if you are going to use the rib cage! If you are just going to "quarter" the meat and use the quarters, tremendous care in this area is not needed.
- Drain all excess blood from the hog. If the hog has been "gut shot" (shot below the diaphragm chest cavity), it is necessary to wash out the carcass with water as soon as possible to prevent meat spoilage.

Removing Hogs from the Field

After field dressing, it is advisable to leave the hide on the hog to protect the meat from dirt and insects while transporting it to the truck. If you are not leaving the woods immediately, cool the carcass as quickly as possible. Find a spot in the shade and prop the body cavity open with a stick to permit air circulation into the opening. This will help release the heat within the body and prolong the time before the meat will spoil. It is important to know that meat will "heat-up" even if the day is somewhat cool. This is a part of the "decomposition" process!

Getting DEAD Hogs out of the Woods!

Getting your hog out of the woods is sometimes quite a chore. Many times while hunting on public lands, I have found myself two creeks and a long haul from the truck. Dragging a 150 lbs. hog is tough work. There are a number of methods I recommend for getting the hog out of the woods.

- Game Hauler - this is a wheelbarrow type device with either one or two wheels. It costs a few bucks but really helps as long as the pulling is over fields or slightly open woods. These devices run between $100-200.
- Masonry Mixing Tub - this is a plastic tub measuring about 2 feet by 3 feet by 8 inches high. I usually attach a rope and use it like a "sled." It pulls easily and is my favorite method of getting a big hog out of the woods. This device can be bought at any Home Depot or well-stocked hardware stores for about $12. It also keeps the back of your hunting vehicle clean and free of blood!
- The simplest method is to get some rope and tie it around the hog's neck, at the other end of the rope tie a short stick (about 1 foot long). Grab the stick and pull like a Clydesdale!

Marquette brothers removing hog from the field!

Getting LIVE Hogs out of the Woods!

- For short pulls over fields, hog-tie the hog and drag him out like you would a dead hog, just place the noose below his front shoulders so he won't choke. His hide is tough enough to do this! You can also put the rope around his snout behind the canines.
- Find a sturdy rod or stick and tie the legs to it. Get a friend and place the rod over each shoulder and away you go. Make sure his head is out of biting or slashing distance. This method also works for dead hogs.
- Or use the Game Hauler listed above!

Boar removing "himself" from the field!

Skinning

Some old-timers testify that leaving the skin on a hog for too long will ruin the taste of the meat. Like the oft-quoted deer hunting advice to take off the tarsal glands to save from ruining meat, this is a myth. The length of time leaving the hide on the hog does not effect the taste, as long as the meat is properly cooled.

- Cut the skin between the ankle bone and the large tendon and place a stick or gambrel to hang the hog in the air. Hang the hog from the rear legs!
- Beginning at the spot where the gambrel is touching the hog, cut a complete circle through the skin, being careful not to cut the tendon.
- Cut the skin up each leg to the tail. Do this from both legs.
- Pull the skin while placing the edge of the knife into the joint where the skin and carcass meet. Slice and pull, slice and pull, this is the way the skin comes off!
- Take the skin off all the way down to the "elbows" of each leg and down to the neck. Work the skin loose from the belly and flank. Always hold the skin tightly, pulling it away from the carcass as you cut. You'll see the best way to take it off as you go! The skin should come off in one complete unit.
- Take care not to allow the hide to touch the skin as this allows hair to get on the meat.
- Once the skin is off the hog, it is now time to make a decision. You can take a whole hog to the butcher, but you need to halve or quarter the hog if you are going to put him into your cooler. I usually don't bother with the "rib cage" because there is so little meat and we don't usually make our own sausage. I therefore only deal with the 4 leg sections if I am butchering the hog for myself, and take the whole hog if someone else is butchering the hog for me. To quarter the animal, you need a hacksaw or branch cutter.

After quartering or halving the hog, I usually take it to the local butcher for aging and cutting up. Get your butcher to "age" the hog for a few days to tenderize the meat Tell the butcher what you want and he will follow your directions. He can turn some of your hog into "jerky" or sausage or even burger. He can cut as much as you want into roasts or steaks, depending upon your preference. He can make chops or give you ribs (although wild hog ribs are very small, a truly large sow might be worth the effort!).

There are times when getting the hog to the butcher is impractical or too expensive. It's important to know what to do at such times. There are a few basic things to do. First, don't try to "age" the hog. Temperature control is so crucial that spoiling your meat is a real possibility. Second, it is good to simply cut the hog up into as many roasts or steaks as possible. There are many "muscles" around each bone. You simply follow the line of muscle, releasing each individual muscle from the whole. After releasing the muscle, cut across the grain to make your steaks or leave the whole muscle for a roast. I like to de-bone all meat that I use. Put the meat in freezer bags and your hog should keep well in the freezer for up to one year.

Practice insures a well-placed shot, a quick kill, and easy cleaning!

I DONT KNOW HOW YOU CAN HUNT A BEAUTIFUL AND ENDANGERED SPECIES.
ENDANGERED?? HECK, THERE'S BILLIONS OF THEM!!
BBQ

From the Ice Box to First Bite

How to Get a Hog from the Freezer to your Mouth!

Chapter Thirteen

- What special preparations need to be made to cook wild hog?
- What are some great recipes for wild hog?
- How do you structure a dinner party so that there are left-overs for your midnight snacks?

My wife Kelly tried one bite of my first hog and refused to eat or cook or have anything to do with another. I too thought that wild hogs were not good table fare. I gave up thoughts of hunting more hogs after this first dinner episode. If a man's woman won't cook the game, then why kill it was how I reasoned. Kelly ate and cooked so much wild game that I shot, that this exception was something I would have to live with.

A year later my family was invited over to the Marquette's for dinner. We were not looking forward to the advertised meal of wild hog. With great reluctance we put a few small polite pieces on our plates. We didn't mind offending Craig, but Lynn was another matter. After the first bite, I was back in line for more before the serving plate emptied! Kelly too was thrilled. This was the leanest, least wild tasting wild game we had ever had! It was then that we began to learn some important secrets for a good meal of wild hog.

PREPARATION FOR COOKING

If you've killed your first hog, get prepared for some great eating. Your friends are really going to be turned-on to wild game and your family is going to now view you as a 'successful' hunter. Your wife may even allow you to hunt more often and be more sympathetic when you occasionally return home empty handed. After reading this book, this will be a rare event, but bringing home this kind of great eating will be worth the wait.

Here is a universal marinade that will help "cure" any wild taste in the meat. To do this:

Mix in a large crock ...

- ***2 cups of vinegar or 1 bottle white wine***
- ***1 large onion chopped***
- ***3 to 4 cloves of garlic***
- ***2 or 3 bay leaves***
- ***Any other of your favorite seasonings***

Add the meat, cover and place in the fridge for 2 to 4 days. After this, discard the marinade and cook the meat in any way that you wish.

COOKING

When cooking wild pig, it is important to remember that it can be used in any of your favorite pork recipes. WILD HOG IS A BETTER MEAT THAN STORE-BOUGHT DOMESTIC HOG! It is a leaner, better tasting meat if prepared properly. There is one major difference. Since wild hog contains so much less fat, you must cook using "wetter" methods or be very careful to not "over-cook" the meat. Because of the parasites in wild hog, it is important to cook the meat completely. This is a careful balance. An internal temperature of 185 is perfect for fresh pork.

Lynn's Foolproof Hog Roast

A MOUTH-WATERING RECIPE

This recipe is the one used in the story at the beginning of this chapter. It turned a "hostile" wife into a wild pork loving sweetheart! If it worked for me, it will work for you.

Preheat oven to 325°. Prepare for cooking up to 4 lbs. of wild hog meat, roasts, loins, chops, or ribs.

Place the following in roasting pan with cover:

- **2 cups beef broth**
- **½ cup red or white wine**
- **3 cloves garlic, minced**
- **1 large onion, cut in large pieces**
- **1 teaspoon thyme**
- **1 teaspoon oregano**
- **½ teaspoon coarse ground pepper**
- **1 teaspoon salt**

Mix all ingredients. Add hog meat. Cover and cook until meat thermometer inserted reaches 185°. A 3 lb. roast usually requires 3 hours cooking time. Remove from oven and slice to serve as a roast. If you prefer, chop or shred the meat and add your favorite barbeque sauce.

South Carolina BBQ Sauce

Here is a recipe that a friend from South Carolina gave me. It is a sauce that has much less tomato than many other sauces and much more spice! It results in delicious wild hog!

Place the following into a large stock pot:

- **3/4 cup of dark brown sugar**
- **3/4 cup Worcestershire sauce**
- **3/4 cup of prepared mustard**
- **1 20 oz. bottle of Heinz Ketchup**

- **2 tablespoons of black pepper**
- **2 tablespoons of Cayenne pepper**
- **1 12 oz. bottle of Progresso Garlic flavored red wine vinegar**
- **1 quart of water**
- **3 cups of white wine**
- **½ cup salt**

Bring all the ingredients in a large stock pot to a boil. Lower the heat to a simmer and cook uncovered for 30 minutes. The sauce can be stored in the refrigerator in jars. NOTE: This can be used as a marinade as well as a BBQ sauce.

When it's time to try your South Carolina BBQ Sauce, the following recipe is great!

Take 4 lbs of chops, roasts, or steaks and 3 cups of SC BBQ sauce, and marinate them in the sauce for at least 6-8 hours. Place the meat in a roasting pan and bake it in the oven at 350 for 1 hour and 15 minutes. Or put on a out-door smoker using charcoal and hickory for 2 to 3 hours. Baste while cooking a couple of times and check for over-cooking!

Sauteed Fillet of Wild Pig

Here is a simple recipe that a friend gave me for a breakfast feast!

Cut thin slices from the leg or roast. Sprinkle with salt and black pepper. Pound these out thin with the back of a large knife or tenderizing mallet. Saute them in a heavy black skillet over a medium heat in butter and oil. Serve with grits, eggs, and biscuits.

If you aren't a Southerner, you might be tempted to skip the grits! If you do, the meal will not be as tasty and the authors of this book will curse all your future hunts!

Wild Hog Chops

Black Forest Style

- **4 tablespoons flour**
- **1/4 teaspoon ground Thyme**
- **3 tablespoons salt**
- **3 tablespoons fresh ground pepper**
- **4-5 thick chops**
- **4-5 whole cloves of garlic**
- **2 tablespoons lard**
- **1 cup of beef stock**
- **2 bay leaves**
- **2 tablespoons white vinegar**
- **2 teaspoons sugar**
- **3/4 cup sour cream**

Preheat oven to 350. Mix flour, thyme, salt, and pepper - dredge the hog meat. Stick a clove in the center of each piece. In a casserole, saute the floured meat in lard. Heat the remaining ingredients in a sauce pan and stir until the liquid is uniform. Pour over meat in casserole, cover with the lid and bake for 1 hour.

This is just a small sampling of what methods of cooking, and what ingredients can be used to cook the wild hog. Feel free to experiment with your favorite pork recipes and you will experience positive responses from all your friends and family that you serve!

HOW TO EAT (LIKE) A HOG

There are several important hints to eating your hog.

INVITE VERY FEW PEOPLE

This leaves more for you at dinner and more for you in the middle of the night when you want some great left-overs. You must calculate the time and money that has gone into each pound of meat. If you've followed the instructions of this book, your cost-per-pound of meat will be much lower than your average hunter, but it will still be astronomical. For this reason, let me ask you one question, "Why should you invite a large group of people, which will surely include a closet animal rights activist, to share in the feast that you and your family have sacrificed so greatly to have?" It seems wiser to invite a few people who are interested in experimenting with wild game.

DON'T INVITE ANY OTHER HUNTERS

There is a great risk in inviting other hunters. Since you are the host, you will have to do one thing that will have a tremendous implication for your dinner party. You will have to allow your hunting guests to tell their hunting stories first, and this will cause you to exaggerate your stories even more than you normally would. If you are a good liar and a long-time experienced hunter, this will be no problem. If, on the other hand, you are a beginning hunter or a poor liar, this will throw you off your pace. This could result in people openly not believing your story. This is a hunters greatest fear!

DON'T FILL YOUR PLATE AT THE FIRST SERVING

Most people will think that you are being "polite", but actually you are making a strategic move to be sure that you get more than others. If you put a smaller first portion on your plate, you can return for a quicker and larger second helping before the others are finished. This also makes you first in line for any potential third helping that you might desire.

REPLAY THE KILLING OF THE HOG TWO OR THREE TIMES DURING THE MEAL!

There are a number of good reasons that this is important. First, the guests must be polite and listen intently because they are eating the "victim." You will never get a more captive audience than this one. Second, for non-hunters, the story itself might slow their eating and leave more for you. As a matter of fact, if you disregard the first tip and invite too many people, this tip might save you a midnight snack!

BE SURE TO EXAGGERATE THE SIZE OF THE HOG AND THE DIFFICULTY OF THE SHOT!

All hunters know that game animals continue to grow after being killed. In a few years, the average hog killed will gain a hundred pounds in the telling of your hunt story. All hunters realize this phenomenon and mentally recalculate anything that is told to them. Non-hunters do not understand this part of hunting culture, so be prepared for the typical question, "If the hog was so big, why was so little hog left after our meal?" If you give an honest answer and reply, "We didn't want to waste too much hog on friends," you will not live up to the polite image you developed by taking a small first portion. The correct answer in this situation is, "The hog I shot wasn't the only pig attending the meal" or "We didn't know you would like wild hog meat."

A Word about Ethics

Chapter Fourteen

We live in a world that is at war over ethical issues: Animal Rights vs. Human Rights; Protection of the Environment vs. Use of the Environment; Individual Property Rights vs. Government Mandated Restrictions. These issues will be before us for as long as we will live upon the planet.

Each person in our world has an opinion about these issues. Those decisions are based upon a personal ethical system that has either been assumed without reflection or carefully developed over time. There seems to be an environmental and man-is-first ethic at battle in our world today.

The Environmental Ethic

Our educational system and culture is assuming some basic elements of an environmental ethic and philosophy.

- All life, especially animal life, is equal upon the planet. "The animals are our brothers" is the common motto.
- Because animals are our brothers and since animals feel pain, hunting animals (or even bothering them) is considered to be one of the worst wrongs. PETA (People for the Ethical Treatment of Animals) just came out against fishing as well as hunting based on this logic.
- The will of the "moral public" takes priority over individuals who disagree with their philosophy or decisions.

Does this philosophy hold up to logic? The philosophy falls short in it's "Disney World" perspective as we look more honestly at the issues.

- **Animals have no "ethic" about killing other animals.**

The oft-quoted environmental proverb that animals only kill to eat is clearly wrong. Some animals enjoy killing and will go out of their way to do so. Animals have no "moral" sense and this separates us from the animals in the most profound ways! If man is only an animal, why should he hold to an ethic that is so against natural habit?

- **Animal rights activists are not consistent with their own philosophy.**

They believe that we all evolved from micro-organisms and thus, we are all equal. Humans just happen to find themselves at a higher rung on the ladder of evolution. Why then is man seen as a separate entity than the animals? Why is it moral and right for predator animals to kill, yet not for man? Man has "canine" teeth and was clearly designed to be a predator. Why should we deny the "nature" within us while animals are encouraged to follow theirs? Especially if our "nature" can be managed so as to benefit wildlife as a whole rather than harming it?

- **Animal rights activists fail to recognize that all human life upon the planet is at the expense of animal life.**

No animal rights activist can live within a home and eat only vegetables without killing animals. Hunters are seen as the enemy, but this is highly inconsistent. The land that I hunt holds the same amount of animals from year-to-year. The average deer, hog, and turkey population remains somewhat constant. I have not harmed these populations but have instead been used as a management tool to make the over-all populations more healthy.

Animal rights activists fail to see that all human life upon the planet takes away animal life. The "vegetables" that the animal rights activist eat for dinner is grown on destroyed wildlife habitat. The home that the animal rights activist lives in was once wildlife habitat too. The difference between the death that animal rights activists (and all humans) cause and the death that hunters cause is this. Wildlife habitat destruction is permanent for the species as a whole, whereas hunting is only permanent for the few individuals killed.

The Man-is-First Ethic

The Man-is-First ethic is almost unarticulated, but clearly the view of many in our society.

- **Humans are the highest animal upon the earth and therefore have the right to do with animals what we will.**
- **The resources upon the planet are the sole possession of the humans who happen to own them.**
- **An individual's right to do with the resources and animals found upon his property supersedes all other interests.**

The results of this ethic are clear - there has been a rape and devastation of the earth. The consequences of this ethic are all around us. In the 1970's, we began to become aware of the vast pollution problem and the terrible destruction that it has caused. Streams that no longer hold fish, animals that are sick and diseased, and the millions of acres of habitat which has been destroyed came more and more into focus. Industrial companies have historically put their own interests and profits above any concern for the planet.

Hunters too have been a part of this. The killing off (extinction) of the passenger pigeon and eastern wolf have been caused almost exclusively by hunters with this ethic. Whales, seals, and even deer (in previous generations) populations, as well as others, have been decimated by this ethic.

It is true that hunters have, in recent years, been the leaders in habitat protection and animal reintroduction. The turkey, deer, and duck populations have been helped and returned to a healthy number, almost exclusively, by the efforts and money of hunters. But we are still confused about a proper ethic.

If we, as hunters or farmers or industrialists, see ourselves as having the sole ownership of the earth, it will inevitably lead to the harming of wildlife and habitat. Our decisions will be based ultimately upon what is best for man! This, in the long run, will cause harm, extinction, and the devastation of the earth that we live on.

THE PROPER ETHIC
A DUAL MANDATE

How did man come to be upon the earth? Did we "evolve" like all other animals? Can there be a "morality" without an absolute law existing in the universe?

Modern evolutionary scientist are currently in great confusion and debate. The top evolutionary scientists are admitting that the fossil record does not prove, explain, or support current evolutionary theory. There are many other problems as well.

As a matter of fact, Dean H. Kenyon, Professor of Biology at *San Francisco State University*, was reinstated to his position at the school after being put on academic probation. It seems that Professor Kenyon had offended many in the academic world by pointing out the great problems of evolutionary theory in his Biology 100 class and teaching his students the view that man is a created rather than evolved creature, supported, not by religious ideas but by information theory and molecular biology.

Kenyon summarizes his teaching method in one of the finest universities of our nation when he says ...

> I ... discuss several problems with evolutionary theory, including the gaps in the fossil record, problems in chemical evolutionary theory, the irreducible complexity of biochemical systems and the lack of an explanation for the origin of genetic information. (Kenyon, *The Washington Times*, January 16, 1994)

The "intermediate" links between species do not exist. Changes within a species can be proven, but jumps from one species to another are totally unsubstantiated. When Darwin began the trek down the evolutionary trail, it was assumed that the fossil record would prove the theory. This pursuit has failed, so much so, that Christian professors in secular universities are being allowed to teach their view and atheistic scientists are admitting to the problems.

If evolutionary theory is in doubt, then what are the other options? I see only one. Man is a created, rather than evolved creature. This is the logical and intellectual foundation upon which I base my belief that there is a God and that He has revealed his truth in the Bible. From this Bible I feel that mankind receives the proper ethic regarding hunting and our responsibility for the environment.

Here are the three main foundations upon which I believe the proper ethic is based.

- **God is the owner of all things on the planet.**

"The earth is the LORD'S, and everything in it, the world, and all who live in it; for he founded it upon the seas and established it upon the waters." Psalm 24:1-2

God, not man, is the owner of the plants and trees and animals that walk upon the earth. He is the owner simply because he created it. He made it, therefore it is his.

This means that man is not the ultimate "owner" of anything. We are only stewards and managers of the creation that God has made. Man is not first, God is first. Because God is the owner, he has the right to determine how the earth and every human living upon it is to live. God writes the "owners" manual to his universe.

- **Man has been given stewardship responsibilities of the creation.**

Man has been created as the highest being on the planet. We are created in the image of God himself. This means that we have the moral nature of God and many of his attributes. God placed Adam in the garden and commanded him to "care" for it. Our ethic in dealing with the earth should not be, "what is best for man?" Instead, it should be, "what is the best and greatest use of God's creation?"

This means that hunters need to protect the whole environment, not just game species and game habitat. Our responsibility covers more than our limited interests. The great diversity of life that God has created upon the earth is to be our concern and responsibility. We are stewards of the whole creation that God has given to us to manage.

- **Man has been given the gift of the earth to use for his own benefit.**

"Then God said, 'Be fruitful and increase in number and fill the earth. The fear and dread of you will fall upon all the beasts of the earth and all the birds of the air, upon every creature that moves along the ground, and upon all the fish of the sea; they are given into your hands. Everything that lives and moves will be food for you. Just as I gave you the green plants, I now give you everything.'" Gen. 9:1-3

God here instructs man that he is "over" all the animals of the earth, they are "given into his hands." These hands are to be caring and managing hands. Only mankind has the power to manage the earth to protect it's rich diversity. No animal can fulfill this role, only man.

God is also clear in stating that man is free to use the animals as food for himself. Was this because man could not live upon vegetable life alone and therefore God "allowed" this? Or was it instead part of the richness of God's blessing to man, to allow him to eat and to enjoy both plant and animal? I believe that the command to eat meat is a recognition of the "image of God" in man as a higher creature, who has been created to both rule and use the creation.

Thus, man has a dual mandate from God. The first mandate is that we are to care for the creation. We are responsible to protect the rich diversity of life that we find upon the planet. We are stewards, not owners, of the world around us. The second mandate is this, we are free to "use" the creation. It was created with the diversity it possesses for our enjoyment and enrichment. It is right and proper for us to use the resources for our benefit, to enjoy hunting and fishing and meat-eating. It is right and proper for us to dig coal and pump oil and develop new technologies. Our use of the earth must always be done with the concept of our responsibility to the earth in the forefront of our thinking.

These two mandates must always be kept in balance. If we over-balance in the direction of "care", we fall into the trap of the environmental ethic which "equalizes" animals with man and reduces man's involvement in the world. If we over-balance in the direction of use, we will selfishly destroy the planet. It is only when we see ourselves as "stewards" of a world owned by God, with a dual mandate, that we will live under the proper ethic!

We believe passing our values onto the next generation is the most effective way to fight the anti-hunting mentality!

The Authors of Wildlife Publishing

Craig Marquette

Craig, originally from Chicago, is a 25 year resident of Sarasota, Florida. Craig has hunted and killed hogs very successfully on public lands. His beautiful wife of 25 years, Lynn, provided him with 4 wonderful children; Zack, Wade, Becca, and Katie. Craig, pictured at right in the photo, is holding his first Eastern, a 2 year old, 18 pound gobbler with an 11 inch beard!

Dave Sturkey

Dave is a former Virginian who has hunted throughout the south, mid-west, and west. He and his beautiful wife Kelly now reside in Sarasota, Florida with their 4 wonderful children; Alexandra, Katie, Ben Lee {named after the famous turkey hunter}, and Abby. Dave is pictured at right with his 26th turkey, a 21 pound Missouri Eastern with a 11 3/4 inch beard.

Hog Hunting Seminars

Craig and Dave are available to bring their humorous and informative wild hog hunting seminar to your hunting club, outdoor show, or landowner/sporting association.

To contact Craig and Dave for scheduling and booking information, write to ...

Wildlife Publishing
622 Whitfield Ave.
Sarasota, FL 34243

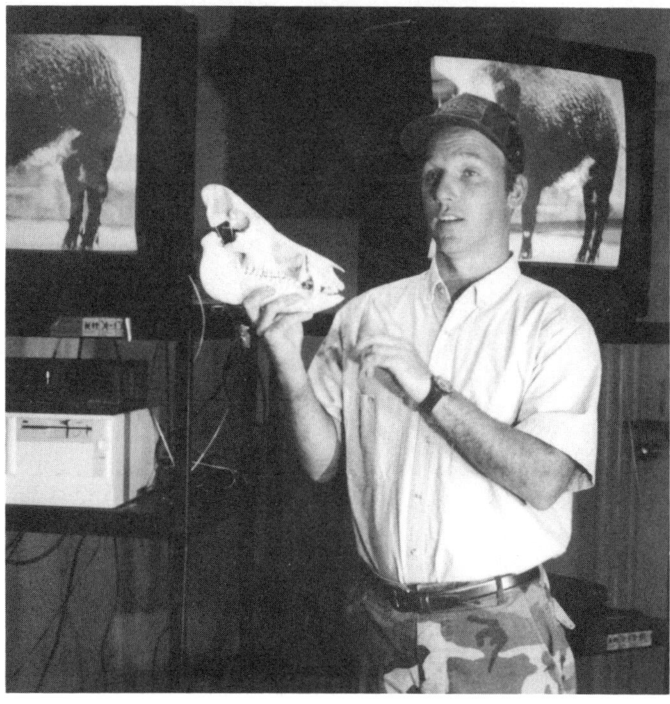

Dave and Craig's multi-media, computer generated, wild hog hunting seminar!

Bibliography

Austin, David H.; Belden, Robert C.; and Frankenberger, William B.; *A Simulated Harvest Study of Feral Hogs in Florida*; 1985.

*Baber, Daniel William; *Social Organization and Behavior in the Feral Hog*; 1976.

Becker, H.N.; Belden, R.C.; Breault, T.; Burridge, M.J.; Frankenberger, W.B.; Nicoletti, Paul; *Brucellosis in Feral Swine in Florida*; 1978.

Creswell, Alfred M.; *Tennessee Feral Hog Report*; Orlando, 1989.

Degner, Robert L.; *Economic Importance of Feral Swine in Florida*; 1989.

Durrance, K.L. and Maxson, C.A.; *Baby Pig Management Practices*; Univ. of Florida.

*Frankenberger, William B. and Belden, Robert C.; *Distribution, Relative Abundance and Management Needs of Feral Hogs in Florida*; 1976; Wildlife Research Laboratory; Gainesville Florida.

*Frankenberger, William B. and Belden, Robert C.; *Management of Feral Hogs in Florida - Past, Present, and Future*; 1977; Georgetown, South Carolina Symposium.

Higginbotham, Dr. Billy; *Feral Hogs: The Good, The Bad or The Ugly?* August 1995.

*Johnson, Philip E.; Law Professor at the Univ. of California, Berkeley; *Darwin on Trial*; Intervarsity Press.

Leek, van der M.L.; Becker, H.N.; Humphrey, C.L.; Belden, R.C.; Frankenberger, W.B.; Nicoletti, P.L.; *Prevalence of Brucella SP. Antibodies in Feral Swine in Florida*; 1993.

*Lewis, C.S.; *Mere Christianity*; Collier Books; New York, NY; 1960.

*Mayer, John J. and Brisbin, I. Lehr; *Wild Pigs in the United States, Their History, Comparative Morphology, and Current Status*; University of Georgia Press; Athens and London; 1991.

PigVision, Inc.; *The Pig's Spectralvision*; 1996.

Robert C. Belden and William B. Frankenberger; *Biology of the Feral Hog Population in South Central Florida*; 1990.

Schmitz, Don C.; *An Assessment of Invasive Non-Indigenous Species in Florida's Public Lands*; Dept. of Environmental Protection, Tallahassee; 1994.

Sue, Dr.; *Fun Facts*; Davis Virtual Market; 1996.

Tate, Jane; *Techniques for Controlling Wild Hogs in Great Smoky Mountains National Park*: Proceedings of a Workshop, Nov. 29-30, 1983.

Taylor, Rick; *The Feral Hog in Texas*; Texas Parks and Wildlife Dept; 1992.

United States Department of Agriculture; *Wild Pigs, Hidden Danger for Farmers and Hunters*; 1991.

United States Department of Agriculture; *African Swine Fever, An Expanding Threat to American Hogs*; 1980.

Walker, W.R. and Myer, R.O.; *Understanding Swine Feeding Programs; Institute of Food and Agricultural Sciences*; Univ. of Florida.

Walker, W.R. and Myer, R.O.; *Types of Swine Diets*; Institute of Food and Agricultural Sciences; Univ. of Florida.

*Authors Recommended Reading

Hog Hunting Guides

The following guides are our advertisers. We wanted to make a place available where you could find a list of reputable guides. We do not have personal knowledge of all of these guides, but we do refer you to chapter 8 on guided hunting as a way to evaluate them. If we do find out that one of our advertisers is a less than professional guide, we will discontinue them from being listed in any future printings.

More Hog Hunting Guides ...

More Hog Hunting Guides ...

More Hog Hunting Guides ...

More Hog Hunting Guides ...